Each volume of

TWENTIETH CENTURY INTERPRETATIONS

presents the best of modern commentary on a
great work of literature, and an original introduction
to that work by an outstanding authority.
Analyzing themes, style, genre,
structural elements, artistic influences,
and historical background, the essays define
the place of the work in its tradition
and make clear its significance for readers of today.

TWENTIETH CENTURY
INTERPRETATIONS
OF
THE ODYSSEY

A Collection of Critical Essays

Edited by

HOWARD W. CLARKE

PRENTICE-HALL, INC. A SPECTRUM BOOK *Englewood Cliffs, N.J. 07632*

Library of Congress Cataloging in Publication Data
Main entry under title:
Twentieth century interpretations of the Odyssey.

    "A Spectrum Book."
    Bibliography: p.
    Includes index.
    1.   Homer.   Odyssey—Addresses, essays, lectures.
I. Clarke, Howard W.
PA4167.T85   1983   883'.01   82-16639
ISBN 0-13-934851-4
ISBN 0-13-934844-1 (pbk.)

10   9   8   7   6   5   4   3   2   1

ISBN 0-13-934851-4

ISBN 0-13-934844-1 {PBK.}

Jacket illustration by Edgar Blakeney
Manufacturing buyer: Barbara A. Frick

Prentice-Hall International, Inc., *London*
Prentice-Hall of Australia Pty. Limited, *Sydney*
Prentice-Hall Canada Inc., *Toronto*
Prentice-Hall of India Private Limited, *New Delhi*
Prentice-Hall of Japan, Inc., *Tokyo*
Prentice-Hall of Southeast Asia Pte. Ltd., *Singapore*
Whitehall Books Limited, *Wellington, New Zealand*
Editora Prentice-Hall do Brasil Ltda., *Rio de Janeiro*

Contents

Introduction

by Howard W. Clarke

The *Odyssey* is Homer's popular epic. The *Iliad* may be more prestigious, but its appeal is limited by its subject, war, by its hero, the proud, vengeful, and introspective Achilles, and by its setting, a bleak and embattled beach before Troy. The *Odyssey* knows no such limitations. Its settings are as varied as its characters, its events as unpredictable as its hero. Its narrative blends materials as diverse as the legends of Troy's fall, the folktales of Odysseus's adventures, and the myths of the returning heroes. And yet with so broad a range, the story's focus remains narrow. The *Odyssey* tells of gods and heroes, with Zeus appearing at the beginning and end and Poseidon stirring up trouble in the middle, and with cameo appearances by Achilles and Agamemnon, Ajax and Nestor, and Helen and Menelaus, but it is Odysseus who dominates the human action, Athena, the divine. In its opening scene Zeus proclaims an ideology of human responsibility and divine concern, but the final message of the poem is reassuringly simple: that, with a modicum of wit and luck, love can endure and courage can prevail. But just barely, and twenty years of separation, the loss of all of Odysseus's companions, and the indiscriminate slaughter of the Suitors remind us that success also has its costs.

The art of Homer in the *Odyssey* is to be inclusive, and his combinations are often startling. Nausicaa may be the princess who lives in a palace with golden doors, but she also does the family laundry, and Calypso may be the enchantress on the faraway isle, but she also has a set of tools on hand for Odysseus to use in building his raft. Odysseus may exemplify the heroic code of personal

I am grateful to the University of Delaware Press for permission to reprint material for this Introduction that appears in my *Homer's Readers: A Historical Introduction to the Iliad and the Odyssey* (Newark, Del.: University of Delaware Press, 1981). Copyright © 1981 Associated University Presses, Inc.

aggrandizement in IX when he calls out his name to the blinded Polyphemus, but he also transcends it in XXII when he cautions Eurycleia not to exult over his defeat of the 108 Suitors. The *Odyssey* may dramatize a masculine world of heroic achievement, but few works in world literature present such remarkable women as prudent Penelope, enterprising Athena, faithful Eurycleia, sweet Nausicaa, frustrated Calypso, ambiguous Circe, even Helen of Troy, now Helen of Sparta and domesticated at last. Its hero's wanderings may belong to the stuff of Greek myth, but so imposing is their quality that many—the Sirens' Song, the Lotus Eaters, Scylla and Charybdis, Circe—have become part of our psychological vocabulary. In their variety they range from the artificial, the Lestrygonians being there mostly because Homer wants to get rid of Odysseus's fleet, to the archetypal, the weak motivation of the Underworld descent suggesting a gravitational pull in heroic myth that is stronger than Homer's narrative needs. And even though the *Odyssey* is largely a poem of common experience, of eating, bathing, clothing, with a hero who has a teenage son and a faithful old dog, many readers sense a more urgent reality beneath the fictive surface: the victory of life over death, variously enacted by Odysseus in surviving multiple threats to his life and returning, first from the land of the dead and then, asleep on a pilotless boat, from the Phaeacians to rescue Penelope and defeat the despoilers of his home.

Called in antiquity "a fair mirror of human life," the *Odyssey* has also mirrored a variety of interpretations. Historically, it was the allegorists who were first and most imaginative, reading Homer's narrative of journey as an instructive metaphor for man's progress through life, with Odysseus as the hero of mind guided by Athena, the goddess of wisdom, or as the human soul beset by this world's perils on its pilgrimage to its true home, heavenly Ithaca. Certainly the atmosphere of the *Odyssey* encourages this approach, for in its world things are not what they seem to be: swineherds are princes and beggars are kings, and it is precisely this gap between what appears to be and what actually is, between what is said and what is meant, that is the basis and justification of allegory. Allegorists also found an obvious inspiration in the person of Proteus, the old man of the sea in IV, who conceals the truth behind a variety of appearances, and so it was in Odysseus's "protean" adventures of V to XII (they generally ignored the second half of the poem) that they sought to discover the various truths of the *Odyssey*. They began with Calypso, the "Concealer," whose mystical role in the poem is to imprison the "soul" of Odysseus in the "matter" of her island, where it is buffeted by the waves of passion, until it can take up the wise man's journey to the "mind" of Penelope. By having Odysseus overcome Polyphemus, Homer teaches us that the fire of intellect can put out the eye of brute nature. Odysseus's difficulties with Aeolus and his bag of winds prove that the winds are our concupiscent appetites that we keep secretly bound within us by the silver cord of virtue, Odysseus's crewmen standing for our senses which, once released from control, turn into storms. For Saint Ambrose the mast to which Odysseus bound himself as he listened to the Sirens' Song was a prototype of the cross of Christ to which the Christian must bind himself when assailed by temptation, Odysseus's ship the Church that bears mankind safely over life's perilous waves. But by far the most rewarding episode was Odysseus's stay with Circe, the temptress who turned his men into animals. The allegorical equivalents seem compelling. Circe is the passion that bestializes, and the *moly* that Hermes gives Odysseus is reason or temperance or eloquence or, for Christian readers, grace. But there are some loose ends in this episode that the allegorists could not easily account for. What, for example, does Odysseus actually do with the *moly*? And would it not have been more instructive morally if Odysseus's crewmen had done something more to deserve their fate than merely accept Circe's hospitality? Should Eurylochus not have received some commendation for being the only one of them all—including wise Odysseus—who wanted nothing to do with Circe? Would it not have been more in keeping with Odysseus's high office if he had not dallied a whole year before yielding to his followers' remonstrances and taking up his return to Penelope? And why did Homer undercut his own allegory by remarking that those whom Circe bewitched were "younger" and "fairer" after recovering their humanity?

It is clear that the allegorists displayed considerable ingenuity. What is less clear is how much their interpretations were part of Homer's purpose. Most critics have not been persuaded. In antiquity Plato, Cicero, and Seneca objected, and in postclassical times Rabelais, Montaigne, and Voltaire (among others) ridiculed their tendency to turn an epic poem into a moralizing guidebook.

But the allegorical approach has not disappeared, and the *Odyssey* continues to deliver messages for the times. These are our times now, and, as befits a self-conscious age, contemporary practitioners read the *Odyssey* as an allegory (a word they choose to avoid) of man's search for identity or struggle for self-awareness, these themes acquiring for many of Homer's current interpreters the vogue that moral didacticism had for the allegorists. The *Odyssey* supports this reading as obligingly as it has so many others. It is a story of a lonely traveler who must win his painful way back to social integration and acceptance as father, husband, and king. Again, it is the adventure books that best dramatize in symbol and narrative the challenges to Odysseus's personality: Poseidon, whose weapon is the anonymous and amorphous sea that would not only destroy Odysseus as a man but would deprive him of any tomb to recall his special greatness; the Cyclops's cave, where Odysseus is "Nobody" until he has overcome brute nature and emerged from its depths with an almost suicidal compulsion to identify himself; Calypso the "Concealer"; the oblivion of the Lotus Eaters and the Sirens; the long delay among the Phaeacians, where, wrapped in borrowed clothes and introduced anonymously to the king and queen, Odysseus, through his exploits in the games and the recollection of his deeds at Troy, acquires the merit that justifies the final disclosure of his identity; and, finally, XXIV, where he is recognized by his father Laertes and confirmed by Athena as descendant of Zeus and king of Ithaca. This completes an allegorical reading that modifies the traditional interpretations, with Odysseus's adventures no longer challenges to his wisdom or tests of his virtue but threats to his identity, his efforts not so much intended to save his life or make his reputation as to preserve his distinctively Odyssean self from subhuman adversaries, reassert it among the Phaeacians, and recreate it, from beggar to king, in the poem's final books. Not what men will think of me, but who I am.

Still, despite its modern recrudescence, the great tradition of Homeric allegory dissolved amid the rationalism of eighteenth-century Europe, as Homer's critics turned from moral and philosophical explication to historical understanding, from a touching faith in Homer the most inspired poet of all time to a critical perspective on Homer the most gifted product of his own time. The seminal work in this transition was a Latin treatise, *Prolegomena ad Homerum* (1795), by a German professor named Friedrich

August Wolf (1759–1824). Wolf's point of departure was simple: how can we be sure that what we read is what Homer created? Wolf decided that we cannot. There was no writing, he claimed, in Homer's time, and the poems are too long to have been composed or preserved without it; there was no occasion for their full recitation and no audience that could absorb such long poems; the lengthy period of oral transmission (for Wolf, 950–550 B.C.) would have totally altered Homer's originals; and so we can hardly expect that our medieval manuscripts have preserved what Homer created. Wolf's solution was to attribute the poems' composition to the so-called Peisistratean Recension, a vague report in a few writers that Peisistratus, an Athenian ruler of the sixth century B.C., "arranged the books of Homer that had previously been scattered" (Cicero), thus removing Homer from responsibility for their final form and assigning it to an anonymous editor or editorial board organized by Peisistratus.

If there was no Homer—at least not for our *Iliad* and *Odyssey*, though he may have composed one or more of the ballads that were later edited into the poems we read—who then is the true source of Homeric genius and artistry? Homer, the first and finest singer of the Trojan saga? Or the rhapsodes, those professional declaimers who took up and adapted his songs for their recitations? Or the collectors and editors who transformed them into our poems? It was the further investigation of these questions—all subsumed now under the "Homeric Question"—that would give rise to a new breed of professional Homerists, mostly German, who would make the poems the property of an academic industry for the next century and a half. This outpouring of scholarship was concerned not so much with meaning as with style and structure, as Wolf's successors analyzed the implausibilities, contradictions, and inconsistencies that they hoped would betray other hands at work on the poems and sought to identify the textual "joins" that would reveal additions and revisions.

Out of the often acrimonious controversies engendered by the Homeric Question there emerged three schools: Unitarians, who feel that the poems we read are substantially what Homer created; Analysts, who feel that the poems are amalgams of one sort or another; and Separatists, who may also be Unitarians or Analysts, but who in any event feel that the *Odyssey* poet is different from the *Iliad* poet. Unitarians have accused Analysts of being pedantic and insensitive, while Analysts have accused Unitarians of ignoring the real difficulties, logical and stylistic, within the poems. For example, Analysts saw in the *Odyssey*'s tripartite organization the possibility that it may once have been a simpler "Return of Odysseus" that was expanded by the addition of the "Telemachy" at one end and the "Vengeance of Odysseus" at the other. They noted, too, that the adventure books are not all of a piece. They fall into three general categories: the quasi-normal episodes of Calypso and the Phaeacians at either end where there is a minimum of folklore material and Odysseus is in little danger of physical harm; the more exotic episodes he recounts to the Phaeacians in X and XII; and, finally, the "Underworld," where Odysseus must interrupt his itinerary for a side trip to the land of the dead. Furthermore, the "Underworld" of XI is not under the world. Odysseus sails across the ocean that, in Homer's geography, flows around the world's perimeter, lands on its other side (which it should not have), performs an appropriate ritual, and summons up whole hordes of ghosts, so there may be a confusion here of two motifs, a trip *down* to Hades and a conjuring *up* of the dead. Odysseus's trip seems poorly motivated, since Teiresias, for all his storied wisdom, does not give him much information about his return, and his mother Anticleia gives him the comforting but quite inaccurate news that Telemachus is living a normal life in Ithaca. Following this, he is treated to a parade of mythical heroines who have no discernible connection with his past or future, and at the end of the book he sees Minos, Tityos, Tantalus, Sisyphus, and Herakles all expiating obscure offenses that have little to do with the *Odyssey*. In the second half of the poem there are a number of apparent anomalies in Odysseus's self-revelation. His disguise seems forgotten in XVII, where his dog Argo recognizes him, and in XVIII, XIX, XX, and XXII, where he does not appear to be the aged and shriveled beggar created by Athena. Some Analysts saw two conflicting versions of the "return" story here, one of an aged hero recognized by signs, such as Odysseus's scar, and another of a hero whose identity is concealed by divine transformation. There may be a similar conflict of versions in XIX, where Odysseus is "pleased" with Penelope's unexpected and implausible decision to show herself to the Suitors and wheedle gifts from them. Could this odd episode reflect a version of Odysseus's homecoming in which Odysseus revealed himself early on to Penelope and then cooperated with her on a plan to defeat the Suitors? Analyst arguments for contaminating versions are strengthened by Penelope's surprising decision to hold the bow contest even though she has just been assured of Odysseus's imminent return. A smaller problem is the fact that the plan Odysseus makes with Telemachus in XVI is not carried out in XIX, since Odysseus abandons the idea of leaving behind weapons for his own use, although he does not yet know that he will be able to use his own bow and arrows. Finally, many Analysts complain about the end of the *Odyssey*, whether it be the abrupt action of XXIV, the almost sadistic scene of Odysseus testing his father Laertes, or the peculiar events of the "Second Underworld" episode.

Unitarians, of course, had their answers to the Analysts' bills of complaint, arguing in general that when Homer seemed to neglect the logic and consistency that Analysts demanded he was after more important poetic or psychological effects. Still, it was easier for Unitarians to belittle or explain away the Analysts' arguments than to refute them, and no one can question the validity, if not the prospects, of Analysts' attempts to find within the *Odyssey* evidence for the process of its creation and transmission. But by the middle of the twentieth century, the polemics of the Homeric Question had generally gone out of fashion, partly because the Analysts had exhausted their arguments without reaching any consensus about how the *Odyssey* was composed or what role in the creative process should be assigned to Homer, but mostly because a new critical approach, generally called the "Parry–Lord Theory of Oral Composition," seemed to render many of their arguments irrelevant. It was the contention of Milman Parry (1902-1935) and his student Albert Lord (1912-   ) that the Homeric poems were oral epics, composed not of words but of formulaic expressions and motifs, and that it was quite possible, though unusual, for a single oral poet to create a poem as long as the *Odyssey*. Parry and Lord based their theory on an analysis of the recurrent combinations of words that strike any reader of the *Odyssey*, even in translation, and they tested their theory in Yugoslavia, where in the 1930s they found a living oral tradition that offered them what they hoped was a model for the creation of Homeric epic. There they discovered illiterate singers who were able to manipulate traditional formulaic expressions and themes with such dexterity that they could develop an extensive repertory of songs and could

even improvise new songs by adapting those already in their repertory.

Oral theory certainly seemed to undermine some of the old approaches, especially the kinds of analyses that assumed a literate
poet or poets collating and revising written texts. Parry and Lord
maintained that it was characteristic of oral poets to assimilate
what they inherited and recreate what they composed and not
simply to stitch together by memory independent poems or parts
of poems that Analyst scholars could unstitch. Their insistence on
the extent and richness of the oral tradition before Homer and on
the improvisational quality of all oral poetry implied that the dis-
crepancies so dear to Analysts' hearts might indicate not a multiplicity of authors and editors but a multiplicity of sources and
themes, each designed to cover a typical narrative situation and
each offering its own stock of formulas and exerting its own
compositional influence within the poem, the theme of the "Aged
Homecomer" conflicting, for example, with that of the "Disguised
King" in the second half of the *Odyssey*. The Yugoslav experience
showed them that composition and recitation are aspects of the
same creative act and that the oral poet is more committed to the
effectiveness of the scene he is immediately presenting to his audience than to establishing its logical relation to other scenes in the
same story. This neatly accounts for the episodic or paratactic
structure of Homeric epic, and if it did not dissolve the inconsistencies and anomalies that had so bedeviled readers since Wolf,
it at least explained how and why some of them had occurred, and
it tended to discount their importance as defects of the poem or as
clues to their composition. On the other hand, those Unitarians
who saw Homer as the original genius conjuring up the *Iliad* and
the *Odyssey* out of his capacious imagination were troubled by the
likelihood that Homer's fabled inventiveness might actually be the
work of generations of mute, inglorious Homers who went before
him and created the repertory of formulaic lines and passages that
Homer drew on in creating his own epics. But in general it seemed
to many Homerists that the Parry–Lord Theory offered a viable
middle way between the Scylla of Unitarian aestheticism and the
Charybdis of Analyst dissection. A compromise seemed possible
that would admit all the Analysts' familiar anomalies but could
account for them in a fashion acceptable to Unitarians, not as the
blunders of an incompetent editor but as the normal compositional

habits of an oral poet manipulating a tradition of inherited phrases, lines, and themes.

One effect of the Parry–Lord Theory has been to revive another aspect of the Homeric Question. Granted that Homer is one poet in a long oral tradition, can we hope to distinguish between the traditional and original components within the poems? What in the *Odyssey* is inherited, what is distinctively Homeric? Telemachus, for example, may be original with Homer. It is difficult to imagine the "Telemachy" existing as an independent poem before the creation of the *Odyssey*. In the poem he plays a most unusual role (Greek mythology is not partial to adolescents), that of a young man being prepared for heroic endeavor, and one can see Homer creating Telemachus as a counterpart to Agamemnon's son Orestes, with whom he is explicitly compared, or even as an improvement, since Orestes could only avenge a dead father whereas Telemachus is able to assist a living father. He would also be an improvement over Odysseus's other son, the Telegonus of post-Homeric poetry, who was born from his relationship with Circe and came to Ithaca, where he unwittingly killed his father. Since the parricide theme is basic to Greek mythology, it is likely that Homer knew this story, just as it is understandable that he wanted to replace Telegonus with a more congenial son and hence created a new and somewhat enigmatic version of Odysseus's death. Because it is important that Telemachus have time to grow up, Odysseus must delay his return home. This he does for seven years with Calypso, whose lack of mythology either in stories outside of Homer or in corroborative details and allusions within the *Odyssey* make her seem very much like Homer's invention. Another purely Homeric figure may be Nausicaa, even though she can also be seen as a type of the king's daughter who will marry the handsome stranger, a milder Medea waiting for her Jason. Indeed, the whole Phaeacian episode, positioned between the fabulous world of the adventures and the realistic world of Ithaca, seems specially fabricated for the immediate narrative needs of the *Odyssey*.

There is also a special part of Homer's world that is not mandated by a tradition. This is his world of things, and readers can look to them not only for clues to his time and place but also as symbols of his poetry. Homer's is a sparsely furnished world, his descriptions are usually formulaic and generalized, and his characters have few material needs, so the objects he does describe tend to draw attention to themselves and in some instances set off emotional resonances. (Readers will have to decide for themselves how much of this symbolism is part of Homer's purpose and how well it coheres with traditional elements of character and action.) In the realm of nature the wild fig tree that Odysseus clings to at the end of XII is no longer growing over the Straits of Messina, but it is only one of a number of trees, usually olive, that assist Odysseus throughout the poem. It is under an olive tree that Odysseus seeks shelter when he crawls ashore on Scheria after his raft is wrecked at the end of V, an olive stake is Odysseus's weapon against Polyphemus, and it is under an olive tree growing on Ithaca's shore that Athena and Odysseus plot their revenge on the Suitors. And, finally, a living olive tree, with all its multiple associations for the Greeks as the gift of Athena, the sign of peace, and the staple of their lives, becomes the great symbol of the *Odyssey* when it is revealed in XXIII that it forms one post of Odysseus's bed. Rooted in the earth yet growing still, it exemplifies the permanence and vitality of Odysseus and Penelope's marriage, and since it is located on the island of Ithaca, it completes the larger symbolic opposition of land and sea, stability and instability, that pervades the entire *Odyssey*. If together they have their bed, to Odysseus belongs his bow as symbol of his power and authority, while Penelope has her shroud, a sign of her loyalty to her father-in-law Laertes, but also a symbol of her resourcefulness in the face of the importunate Suitors.

Even the basic realities of food and warmth acquire symbolic dimensions in the *Odyssey*. The uses of food range in suggestiveness from hunger to hospitality, from cannibalism to carousal, and Odysseus is famished throughout most of the poem. It is both ironic and appropriate, then, that he choose a banquet, that traditional symbol of peace and order, to dispatch the gluttonous and disorderly Suitors. As they lie in XXIII amid the food they had squandered in life, Homer compares their corpses to fish lying on the sand, the life baked out of them by the shining sun. Here Odysseus is associated with the bright sun, his return coming after the long night of the Suitors' anarchy, just as in XVIII and XIX he is associated with the fire that warms, illuminates, cleanses. Odysseus insists on tending the fire during the last evening before the Suitors' deaths, it is by the light of the hearth fire that

Eurycleia recognizes him, and it is fire that he uses in XXII to fumigate his palace and purge it of the Suitors' spilt blood.

So it seems that despite the allegorists' insistence on the *Odyssey*'s homiletic function or the Analysts' insistence on its composite structure or the oralists' insistence on its traditional style, most modern readers still sense within the poem, particularly in translation, the presence of a single and creative genius, whom it is at least convenient to call Homer. These readers, coming to the *Odyssey* with their literary sensibilities shaped by English poetry and fiction, will probably read it less as a classical epic or as a comic counterpart to the tragic *Iliad* than as a romance (the hero's adventures in wonderland) or a novel (the domestic drama in Ithaca). Many may be initially put off by some of the Homeric conventions—the literary style, with its stock epithets, repeated formulas, and lengthy similes; the intervention of the gods; the lack of authorial comment or overt psychologizing. But they will find that they can easily adjust to the world of the *Odyssey*. Homer's formulaic style, for example, provides a stabilizing frame and background for his hero's precarious career, just as the similes illuminate specific scenes by referring them to the larger realities of everyday life. The gods may occasionally seem officious, but their presence adds an increase of power to the story—Athena is Odysseus writ large—and their activities are never so intrusive or arbitrary as to dislocate the human action. And if it is Homer's way to be self-effacing, to dramatize and not analyze, the effect of this technique is to objectify his narrative and lend it credibility. So most readers will soon recognize that Homer's world is, after all, their own, a world of love and lust, of courage and cowardice, a world where the obliviousness of the Lotus Eaters ever opposes the obligations of Ithaca. It is this universality, so characteristically Greek, that has preserved Homeric poetry through shifts of critical fashion and has made the *Odyssey* the most accessible of the ancient classics for the modern reader

To facilitate readers' access to the *Odyssey* is the purpose of this collection of essays. All except Eckert's are by professional classicists, most of whom are also Homerists, and none is available in other anthologies of *Odyssey* scholarship. Lattimore's introduction to his splendid translation briefly surveys all aspects of the poem. Eckert looks at the "Telemachy" from an anthropological perspective. Stanford describes the special qualities of Odysseus's heroism. Using the testimony of Greek pottery styles, Whitman notes the changes in the *Odyssey* that persuade him to date it around 700 B.C. Griffin deals with the complaint that Homeric figures are inadequately characterized. Both Combellack and Wender operate within the Homeric Question, the former analyzing the problem of the Bow Contest and the latter defending the controversial end of the *Odyssey*.

Readers of these essays (and of the translated *Odyssey*) should be aware of the inconsistent spelling of Greek names: Circe/Kirke; Aeolus/Aiolos; Phaeacians/Phaiakians, etc. Some writers prefer the former, or traditional, spellings that have come down through Latin poetry; others, the direct transcription from the Greek; still others keep the traditional spellings for the main characters (Athena, Eurycleia) and use literal spellings for the secondary (Alkinoös, Antikleia).

Introduction to *The Odyssey of Homer*

by Richmond Lattimore

The Outline of the Odyssey

The *Odyssey* as we have it is an epic of over twelve thousand lines. It has been divided, like the *Iliad* and probably at the same time, into twenty-four books. Book number and line number are the standard terms of reference.

The contents can be, very broadly, divided as follows:

The Telemachy or Adventures of Telemachos, i–iv

The Homecoming of Odysseus, v–viii and xiii.1–187

The Great Wanderings, ix–xii

Odysseus on Ithaka, xiii.187–xxiv.548.

We can also distinguish a Proem, Book i.1–10, and an End of the *Odyssey*, all of Book xxiv. This division is for convenience; it is arbitrary and not water-tight, but gives us terms to work with.[1]

I begin by summarizing the bare facts of the story. Odysseus spent ten years fighting at Troy, and another ten years getting home. During this time, none of his family knew what had hap-

---

From the Introduction, pp. 1–22 in *The Odyssey of Homer: A Modern Translation* by Richmond Lattimore. Copyright © 1965, 1967 by Richmond Lattimore. Reprinted by permission of Harper & Row, Publishers, Inc.

[1] It may seem unreasonable to distinguish the Great Wanderings (Troy to Kalypso's island) from the Homecoming (Kalypso's island to Ithaka). The reason for the distinction is Homer's way of recounting these two stages. The Great Wanderings are told by Odysseus in the first person; the Homecoming by the poet in his own person. This makes a great difference. For instance, when Odysseus is made to report divine intervention unseen by him, he has to find a plausible explanation (xii.389–390); when the poet tells the story in his own person, he can do as he pleases. Thus the change of technique, if nothing else, puts the two stages of wandering on different levels.

pened to him, and he lost all his ships, all his men, and the spoils from Troy. After ten years, or in the tenth year, he was set down in his own country, alone and secretly, though with a new set of possessions, by the Phaiakians of Scheria, who were the last people he visited on his wanderings.

When he took ship for Troy, Odysseus left behind his wife, Penelope, and his infant son, Telemachos. A few years before his return, the young bachelors of Odysseus's kingdom, Ithaka and the surrounding islands, began paying court to Penelope (ii.89–90). She was accomplished and clever, still beautiful, an heiress and presumably a widow; but she clung to the hope that Odysseus might come back, and held them off, without ever saying positively that she would never marry again.

The suitors made themselves at home as uninvited guests in the palace of Odysseus. Shortly before the return of Odysseus, Telemachos visited the mainland in search of news about his father. He heard from Menelaos that Odysseus was alive but detained without means of return on the island of Kalypso (iv.555–560). Telemachos returned to Ithaka. The suitors set an ambush, meaning to murder him, but he eluded them and reached Ithaka just after his father arrived.

The voyage of Telemachos, the arrival of Odysseus, and the recognition and reunion of father and son, were all supervised by Athene.

Father and son plotted the destruction of the suitors. Odysseus entered his own house unrecognized, mingled with the suitors and talked with Penelope. He and Telemachos contrived to catch them unarmed and with the help of two loyal serving men (and of course Athene) they slaughtered all 108 suitors. Penelope knew nothing of the plot; Odysseus revealed himself to her after the fighting was over. The relatives of the dead suitors attacked the heroes on the farm of Laertes, father of Odysseus, and a battle began, but it was ended by Zeus and Athene, who patched up a hasty reconciliation.

The Telemachy

The *Odyssey*, like the *Iliad*, begins in the tenth year of the story's chief action, with events nearing their climax and final solution. We begin with a very rapid location of Odysseus in place, time, and stage in his career, but then (via the councils of the gods concerning his immediate fate) pass to Telemachos, with Athene's visit which sends him off on his journey. It is only after Telemachos has begun his visit in Sparta, and heard from Menelaos that his father is alive, and after the suitors have set their trap, that we return directly to Odysseus himself. We then follow Odysseus for the rest of the *Odyssey*. The poet now tells us of Odysseus's journey to Scheria and his sojourn there; and he makes Odysseus himself recount to the Phaiakians his previous wanderings (The Great Wanderings). They then convey him to Ithaka, and with his homecoming the tale of the wanderings of Odysseus joins on to the tale of Odysseus on Ithaka.

Thus in two respects the narrative order of the poem disagrees with the chronological order of the story. The early and chief wanderings of Odysseus are told by throwback narrative toward the middle of the poem; and the wanderings of Telemachos come first.

The joins or transitions from theme to theme are noteworthy. After the poet has located Odysseus in time and space, the gods consider the question. Athene urges the homecoming of Odysseus. Zeus proclaims that Athene shall have her way; Odysseus may now start for home. Athene answers (i.81–95)

> Son of Kronos, our father, O lordliest of the mighty,
> if in truth this is pleasing to the blessed immortals,
> that Odysseus of the many designs shall return home, then
> let us dispatch Hermes, the guide, the slayer of Argos,
> to the island of Ogygia, so that with all speed
> he may announce to the lovely-haired nymph our absolute purpose,
> the homecoming of enduring Odysseus, that he shall come back.
> But I shall make my way to Ithaka, so that I may stir up
> his son a little, and put some confidence in him
> to summon into assembly the flowing-haired Achaians,
> and make a statement to all the suitors, who now forever
> slaughter his crowding sheep and lumbering horn-curved cattle;
> and I will convey him into Sparta and to sandy Pylos
> to ask after his dear father's homecoming, if he can hear something,
> and so that among people he may win a good reputation.

This excellently motivates the Telemachy but it does perforce leave Odysseus stranded, and after the major part of the Telemachy, at the opening of Book v, the return to Odysseus shows more strain

than the departure from him did. Athene has been to Ithaka, and
to Pylos with Telemachos. She left the court of Nestor, presumably
for Olympos (iii.371). Now she has to start all over again, almost
as if the case of Odysseus had never come up, to complain of his
sorrows; but ends with the perils of Telemachos; and Zeus seems
to have to remind her that she herself planned everything that has
just been happening (v.23). Hermes, who has been waiting for this
for four books and five days, can at last get off (i.84; v.28) and the
wanderings of Odysseus may be resumed.

The obviousness of the joins and the bulk of material not
specifically related to Odysseus in Books iii–iv, his absence from
Books i–ii, have suggested that the Telemachy was an independent
poem which was, at some stage, incorporated more or less whole
in the *Odyssey*.[2] This may be true, and there is no way to prove
that it is not true. But it is also possible that the poet (or poets)[3]
of the *Odyssey*, in the form in which we have it, deliberately
developed this diversion, never meaning to take up Odysseus until
he had first established Telemachos; that he so much desired to do
this that he was willing to accept the necessary awkwardnesses of
narrative joining in which it would involve him.

Why so? Let us consider the effects gained for the total poem
from having the Telemachy with its present contents in its present
place.

Odysseus in the *Iliad* was a great man, but his magnitude is increased by the flattering mentions of him by Nestor (iii.120–123),
Menelaos (iv.333–346), and Athene herself (i.255–256 with 265–
266). It is increased still more by the evident need for him felt by
his family and friends, concisely stated by Athene (i.253–254):
"How great your need is now of the absent Odysseus," and everywhere apparent.

Through Nestor and Menelaos, also, the *Odyssey* is secured in
its place among the *Nostoi*,[4] the homecomings of the Achaians.

---

[2] See D. L. Page, *The Homeric Odyssey* (Oxford, 1955), p. 53; for a contrary view, G. S. Kirk, *The Songs of Homer* (Cambridge, 1962), pp. 358–360.

[3] I believe in one poet. There may have been more. Having said so much, I
shall henceforth speak of "the poet." There may, indeed there must, be in-
terpolated lines and passages. I do not know which ones they are.

[4] By the *Nostoi* I mean, not the post-Homeric poem called *Nostoi* or
returns, but the underlying material, traces of which are to be found in the
Odyssey itself.

The general character of the *Nostoi* is succinctly stated by Nestor (iii.130–135):

> But after we had sacked the sheer citadel of Priam,
> and were going away in our ships, and the god scattered the Achaians,
> then Zeus in his mind devised a sorry homecoming
> for the Argives, since not all were considerate and righteous;
> therefore many of them found a bad way home, because of
> the ruinous anger of the Gray-eyed One, whose father is mighty.

The sufferings of two great heroes, by long wandering away from home (Menelaos) and by treachery and disaster on arrival (Agamemnon), both well point up the case of Odysseus in two of its different aspects. For an audience well versed in the tale of Troy, or the *Iliad*, interest is added in a second viewing of some old favorites: Nestor, Helen, Menelaos, all very like themselves in the *Iliad*. Without planning some such excursus as the Telemachy, the poet could not have worked them in without a great deal more awkwardness than it has, in fact, cost him.

Another point gained through the Telemachy is the instigation to murder.

For Odysseus must end by murdering Penelope's suitors. So, it appears, the story demanded. Further, the story demanded, or the poet firmly intended, that Telemachos should assist his father in this business. The suitors are a bad lot and they have put themselves in the wrong, but we cannot assume that Homer's audience was so inured to bloodshed that they could take this altogether lightly (modern readers mostly cannot). In any case, there are numerous passages in the Telemachy which look as if they might be designed, which do in any case serve, to shore up the consciences of the avenging heroes and of their sympathizers in the story or in the audience.

Aigisthos seduced Agamemnon's wife while he was gone at Troy and murdered him on his return. Orestes murdered his father's murderer. The case may not seem quite parallel to the situation of the *Odyssey*, but Agamemnon's ghost used his story as a warning against the wife's-suitor danger (xi.441–446; 454–456); and when Athene tells Odysseus about Penelope and her suitors he immediately thinks of Agamemnon (xiii.383–385). Orestes' act seems to be taken as a precedent justifying murder when it means putting one's house in order. It is mentioned with approval by Zeus (i.35–43), and Athene specifically holds up Orestes as an example to Telemachos (i.298–300). Nestor tells Telemachos of Orestes' revenge, and immediately warns Telemachos not to stay too long away from home—once again, as if there were a specific connection (iii.306–316).

It is not only through her praise of Orestes that Athene shows, at the very outset of the *Odyssey,* that she favors, one might even say insists on, the slaughter of the suitors. She definitely tells Telemachos to do it (i.294–296). And in order that they may be the more guilty, she has apparently put the plot of ambushing Telemachos into their minds, while at the same time making sure that it must fail (v.23–24). The whole later action of the *Odyssey* is approved, authorized, encouraged by Athene.

She is carefully established in this role at the outset of the epic as we have it. This, I believe, is the chief reason why we start with the Telemachy. Here she can be cast as the fairy godmother, or guardian spirit. If the poet had begun at the beginning of the wanderings of Odysseus, he could not have cast her in this role, be-cause the tradition was that at this time Athene was angry with all the Achaians, including even Odysseus. So, for instance, Phemios sang of (i.326–327)

> the Achaians' bitter homecoming
> from Troy, which Pallas Athene had inflicted upon them.

Nestor agrees, adding the wrath of Zeus (iii.130–135 quoted above).

The wrath of Athene deserves special consideration, and I shall return to it when I discuss the wanderings of Odysseus. Here it may be sufficient to say that the poet has established the position of Athene, as guardian spirit of the family, by beginning with the Telemachy.

Last of all, and most obvious of all, the Telemachy gives us Telemachos. Once Odysseus is on the scene, our attention is mainly fixed on him, but his young helper quietly maintains the character that has been built up for him, without strain or hurry, in the first four books.

I think, then, that it can be said, as objectively as is possible in such cases, that the *Odyssey* gains much from its Telemachy. The cost is the delay in bringing us, first-hand, to Odysseus and his wanderings. But did Homer count such delay as cost?

In the *Odyssey*, the poet gives us a few indications of his views about storytelling. One should not be repetitive, xii.450–453:

> Why tell the rest of
> this story again, since yesterday in your house I told it
> to you and your majestic wife? It is hateful to me
> to tell a story over again, when it has been well told.

And well has Odysseus (Homer, that is) told his story. Thus Alkinoös, xi.366–368:

> You have
> a grace upon your words, and there is sound sense within them,
> and expertly, as a singer would do, you have told the story.

It is storytelling they like, and they are not impatient, xi.372–376:

> Here is
> a night that is very long, it is endless. It is not time yet
> to sleep in the palace. But go on telling your wonderful story.
> I myself could hold out until the bright dawn, if only
> you could bear to tell me, here in the palace, of your sufferings.

"If you could only hear him," says Eumaios to Penelope. "I had him for three nights, and he enchanted me" (xvii.512–521).

Delay, excursus, elaboration—whether by creative expansion or incorporation of by-material—is part of the technique of the epic, as opposed to chronicle. In the *Iliad*, the wrath of Achilleus is not hastened to its fulfillment; nor, in the *Odyssey*, the vengeance of Odysseus. Consider the daydream of Telemachos, how he visualizes his father's homecoming, i.115–116:

> imagining in his mind his great father, how he might come back
> and all throughout the house might cause the suitors to scatter.

All he has to do is appear, armed, and the suitors will scatter in panic. So too Athene, i.255–256; 265–266:

> I wish he could come now to stand in the outer doorway
> of his house, wearing a helmet and carrying shield and two
> spears. . . .

> I wish that such an Odysseus would come now among the suitors.
> They all would find death was quick, and marriage a painful
> matter.[5]

Over too quickly, a tableau, not a story. How different is the actual
return and slow-plotted slaying, directed by Athene herself. Delaying matter, if worthy, was, I think, welcome.

The Wanderings of Odysseus

The wanderings themselves can be considered under four headings, as follows.

a. The Wanderings as part of the *Nostoi,* or general homecoming of the
   Achaians.

b. The Great Wanderings, from Troy to Kalypso's isle, recounted to the
   Phaiakians by Odysseus himself, Books ix-xii.

c. The Homecoming, from Kalypso's isle to Ithaka, including the stay with
   the Phaiakians. This is told by the poet as narrator, not by Odysseus,
   and occupies Books v-viii, and xiii.1-187, being interrupted by Odysseus's account of the Great Wanderings.

d. The lying stories told by Odysseus when he is disguised as a tramp
   pretending to be a fallen noble; together with some information which
   Odysseus as tramp claims to have heard about the true Odysseus.

a. The Wanderings of Odysseus are placed among the general
homecomings, or *Nostoi* (the subject of a later epic) at the very
outset, i.11-14:

> Then all the others, as many as fled sheer destruction,
> were at home now, having escaped the sea and the fighting.
> This one alone, longing for his wife and his homecoming,
> was detained by the queenly nymph Kalypso, bright among
> goddesses.

Elsewhere in the first four books we have scattered allusions to the
homecomings. They are generally characterized by Nestor's speech,
iii.130-135:

> But after we had sacked the sheer citadel of Priam,
> and were going away in our ships, and the god scattered the
> Achaians,

[5] Menelaos speaks in the same vein, iv.332-345.

> then Zeus in his mind devised a sorry homecoming
> for the Argives, since not all were considerate nor righteo
> therefore many of them found a bad way home, because
> the ruinous anger of the Gray-eyed One, whose father is mig....

We are told of the murder of Agamemnon, the wreck and drowning of Aias Oïleus, the storm battering and wanderings of Menelaos. Yet there is sometimes an odd note of inconsistency. Nestor reports that he and Diomedes came home without mishap, and that he has heard that Neoptolemos, Philoktetes, and Idomeneus did the same.[6] Proteus tells Menelaos that only two chiefs perished in the homecoming (iv.496–497). This does not square very well with the "sorry homecoming" spoken of by Nestor and mentioned elsewhere, nor does Nestor's account of the departure of Odysseus agree well with Odysseus's own account.[7] It is possible that there was an early variant version of the *Nostoi*.

b. and c. The Great Wanderings, starting from Troy, take Odysseus to the Kikonians, the Lotus-Eaters, the Cyclopes, Aiolos, the Laistrygones, Circe's isle, the Land of the Dead, the Sirens, Skylla and Charybdis, Thrinakia, and Kalypso's isle. From the Kikonians he is driven south, off the map, and his last certainly identifiable landmark is Kythera (ix.81). After that, except for a brief sight of Ithaka (x.28–55), he wanders among marvels, and though his seas and landfalls have often been identified, all is hypothetical and nothing is secure.

Through these adventures, partly perhaps because Odysseus is telling them in his own person, the major gods appear very little. Athene does not appear at all. Responsibility for the troubled wanderings is pinned on Poseidon through the prayer of Polyphemos, his son, after his blinding (ix.528–536).

[6] iii.180–192. It is interesting that for all these heroes, except Nestor, later variants had them either not reach home at all (Neoptolemos) or else wander after their homecomings. Both Diomedes and Idomeneus barely escaped the fate of Agamemnon. For Neoptolemos, see Pindar, *Sixth Paean;* for Idomeneus, see the late compilation of Apollodorus, edited and translated by J. A. Frazer (London and Cambridge, Mass., 1921), vol. ii, p. 249, and for Philoctetes, p. 257. For Diomedes, see the material in H. J. Rose, *A Handbook of Greek Mythology* (New York, 1959), p. 237.

[7] According to Nestor, Odysseus set off in his company, but then turned back with some others (who? how many?) to rejoin Agamemnon (iii.162–164). Odysseus says nothing about this; in his own story he simply sets off from Ilion by himself, with his own contingent. There is no outright contradiction; there is certainly a gap.

Here, as we have noted, the order in the epic narrative does not follow the chronological order. The invocation and the opening scene, before leading to the Telemachy, established Poseidon as the persecutor of Odysseus, i.68–79 (Zeus speaking):

> It is the earth encircler Poseidon who, ever relentless,
> nurses a grudge because of the Cyclops, whose eye he blinded;
> for Polyphemos like a god, whose power is greatest
> over all the Cyclopes. Thoösa, a nymph, was his mother,
> and she is daughter of Phorkys, lord of the barren salt water,
> who in the hollows of the caves had lain with Poseidon.
> For his sake Poseidon, shaker of the earth, although he does not
> kill Odysseus, yet drives him back from the land of his fathers.
> But come, let all of us who are here work out his homecoming,
> and see to it that he returns. Poseidon shall put away
> his anger; for all alone and against the will of the other
> immortal gods united he can accomplish nothing.

Poseidon is Odysseus's persecutor, just as Athene is firmly established as his protector (i.48–62).

The Telemachy follows, and then the Homecoming, which as we have seen starts with Athene taking up the case of Odysseus. She helps him against Poseidon, who wrecks his raft and who proposes to take a final revenge on the Phaiakians for conveying him home. It looks like contrivance; at least, the result is to mitigate any tradition that the sufferings of Odysseus and the other Achaians were due to the wrath of Athene.

The hallmark of the wanderings, from Troy to home, is imaginative combination.

` Except for the very beginning, known places do not figure; nor traditional characters, except in the Land of the Dead. The gods of Olympos, I have said, are not prominent. Rather, we see much of minor divinities, ill-attested outside of the *Odyssey* itself, such as Circe and Kalypso. We find monsters like Skylla and Charybdis, and the delightful but almost equally monstrous Sirens. We have mortals who are almost superhuman in one dimension or another. The Lotus-Eaters offer magic fruit (ix.92–97). The Phaiakians have their magic ships (viii.555–563), they may even have automatons (vii.91–94; 100–102),[8] their orchards bear fruit forever in season

---

[8] Hephaistos in the *Iliad* also has automatons; see *Iliad* XVIII. 376–377; 417–420. But Hephaistos is a god, and the Phaiakians are mortal men.

and out (vii.114–126), and the gods, who live near them, visit them openly without disguise (vii.201–206). The Laistrygones have supernatural strength and ferocity (x.116–124), and the normal seasons do not seem to apply in their country.

Consider also Aiolos. He lives a blissful life in a brazen tower with his six sons married to his six daughters (x.1–2), and in flat contradiction to epic tradition elsewhere, he, a mortal, has been put by Zeus in charge of all the winds, whom he keeps tied up in a bag.

So, too, the Cyclopes of the *Odyssey* are quite different from the Cyclopes in Hesiod and elsewhere. Elsewhere they are gods: in the *Odyssey* they are mortals. Elsewhere there are three of them, and their names are Brontes, Steropes, and Arges; in the *Odyssey* they are apparently numerous, and one of them is named Polyphemos; this Polyphemos is the son of Poseidon, but elsewhere the Cyclopes are the sons of Ouranos and Gaia. Elsewhere they are smiths and builders, but in the *Odyssey* they are herdsmen, or at least Polyphemos is. Their chief and perhaps sole similarity is the single eye, and the name of Cyclops.[9]

Now Cyclops (Kyklops) means not "one-eyed" but "round-eyed." Thus Hesiod, not content with the name, describes them as being not merely round-eyed but one-eyed, *Theogony* 142–145:

> These in all the rest of their shape were made like gods,
> but they had only one eye set in the middle of their foreheads.
> Kyklopes, Wheel-eyed, was the name given them, by reason
> of the single wheel-shaped eye that was set in their foreheads.

Homer, on the other hand, while describing their nature and way of life, never tells us that they are one-eyed, but seems rather to assume that Polyphemos is one-eyed, or rather that we know he is. This comes up when Odysseus proposes to blind him, ix.331–333:

> Next I told the rest of the men to cast lots, to find out
> which of them must endure with me to take up the great beam
> and spin it in Cyclops's eye when sweet sleep had come over him.

The blinding scene which follows assumes throughout that there is only one eye to deal with.

---

[9] For the Cyclopes, see Hesiod, *Theogony*, 139–146; see further the brief and clear account of Rose, *op. cit.*, p. 22.

This suggests to me that Homer "borrowed" the name and the notion of Cyclops for his story and that the name Cyclops by now "meant," that is implied, a one-eyed giant. The story itself may have been a previous folk tale, since it has many analogies;[10] or it may have been free invention. Be that as it may, the story of the blinding of Polyphemos the Cyclops as we have it brings Poseidon into the story. His prayer to his father (ix.526–536) causes the troubled wanderings of Odysseus, as we were told at the start (i.68–75) and elsewhere. But Odysseus at the time of the blinding was *already* lost from home; his wanderings were begun before they were caused.

The paradox seems most plausibly explained as a compromise. Homer knew and admitted the wrath of Athene (and Zeus and other gods)[11] which caused suffering to the Achaians, including Odysseus. But he alters it as far as he can to a situation where Athene merely acquiesces in the sufferings of Odysseus out of respect for Poseidon, whose wrath is thus emphasized.

On Ithaka, Odysseus gently complains to Athene that, while he enjoyed her patronage at Troy and among the Phaiakians, he did miss her company in between, that is, on the Great Wanderings (xiii.314–323). She ultimately answers this, xiii.339–343:

> And I never did have any doubt, but in my heart always
> knew how you would come home, having lost all of your companions.
> But, you see, I did not want to fight with my father's
> brother, Poseidon, who was holding a grudge against you
> in his heart, and because you blinded his dear son, hated you.

Perhaps this will stand as Athene's official version.

d. In addition to the authentic wanderings of Odysseus recounted by the hero himself or by the poet, there are five false stories told by the hero about himself. These are addressed respectively to Athene (xiii.256–286), Eumaios (xiv.191–359), the suitors (xvii.419–444), Penelope (xix.165–202), and Laertes (xxiv.301–308). All the stories serve as answers to the standard question,

---

[10] Conveniently summarized by Frazer in an appendix to his translation of Apollodorus (cited above, note 6), vol. ii, pp. 404–455.

[11] We may instance the wraths, against Odysseus or other Achaian heroes, of Helios, i.9; xii.376; of Zeus and Helios, xix.276; of Zeus, iii.132, 152, 160, 288; ix.38, 552–555; xii.415; of Athene, i.327; iii.135; iv.502; v.108.

spoken or unspoken, raised by the presence of a stranger (especially on an island): "Who are you and where do you come from?" All the stories involve known and identifiable places. They are meant to be plausible, and the supernatural and the marvelous elements of the wanderings find no place here.

The longest and fullest account is the second, given to Eumaios. Here Odysseus represents himself as a Cretan, a veteran of the Trojan War, who subsequently led a disastrous raid on Egypt, was spared and befriended by the Egyptian King, survived the wreck of a Phoenician ship, and came to Ithaka by way of Thesprotia. The first, third, and fourth accounts vary or repeat these themes. All the first four necessarily represent Odysseus as a former nobleman down on his luck. By the time he talks to Laertes, however, he has recovered his property and status, and the story of the fallen noble is no longer necessary. He is from Alybas, wherever that may be, and has arrived from Sikania, presumably Sicily.

The story of the raid on Egypt has attracted special attention. It reads like an account of one of the great raids by the Peoples of the Sea, attested in the annals of Egypt, but told here from the invaders' point of view.[12] This would tie the Homeric poems to history, and suggest that the tradition of troubled homecomings for the Achaians might have originated in actual turbulence and wanderings after the Trojan War.

The presence of these stories in the final version of the *Odyssey* could perhaps be accounted for by the poet's desire to exploit and develop the talents of his hero, giving content to the general comment, xix.203:

> He knew how to say many false things that were like true sayings.

But it is also possible that the lying stories, taken together, might represent a fragmentary outline of an original *Odyssey*, in which the wanderings were confined to known places in the Mediterranean: Crete, Cyprus, Egypt, Phoenicia, Thesprotia; and which the present *Odyssey* has replaced. One could thus make up a rough and imperfect series of analogies, such as, for instance:

Raid on Egypt	Great Wanderings
Egyptian counterattack	Laistrygones

---

[12] See Kirk, *op. cit.*, pp. 41–43.

King of Egypt	Circe or Kalypso
Phoenician wreck	Wreck of Odysseus's last ship or of the raft
Thesprotia	Scheria, the land of the Phaiakians

Nothing like this can, of course, be pressed, but the lying stories in themselves emphasize the element of imagination in the *Odyssey* as we have it. By contrast to the Great Wanderings, the lying stories link rather to the *Nostoi.*

The World of the Wanderings

The world of the Wanderings has occasioned even more controversy. Briefly, there are two extreme views. On the one, the places in the Wanderings, such as the land of the Lotus-Eaters, Circe's Isle, Scheria, and so forth, represent real places in the Mediterranean, or even out of it; or at least some of them do. On the other view, they are imaginary. Both these views seem indeed to be extreme, but it is difficult to find a middle ground.

Many identifications have been made, and the whole subject is too large and complicated to treat in detail.[13] It may be useful to look at a few favorite identifications. The Lotus-Eaters are regularly located on the coast of Libya (Africa), because of the sailing log, though Homer, who knows of Libya, does not use the name here. There is a strong tradition that places Polyphemos and the Cyclopes in Sicily. Skylla and Charybdis have often, despite many objections, been located in the Straits of Messina. Korkya (now often called Corfu) claimed to be Scheria, the land of the Phaiakians.

Some of these traditions are early. Thucydides, writing at the end of the fifth century B.C., refers to legends about Cyclopes, and also Laistrygones, in Sicily, and to the Korkyraians' pride in the ancient sea fame of the Phaiakians.[14] Also, the traditions have survived, or have been resuscitated, and to this day near Acireale the Sicilians will show you the rocks Polyphemos threw at the ship of

[13] See W. W. Hyde, *Ancient Greek Mariners* (New York, 1947), pp. 72–98. This is an excellent concise account of identifications, ancient and modern, made for sites and landmarks in the *Odyssey.* It needs, however, to be brought up to date.

[14] For Sicily, see Thucydides vi.2.1; for Korkyra, i.25.4.

Odysseus,[15] while at Corfu your guide will point out the little island which is the Phaiakian ship turned to stone, and the bay where Odysseus encountered Nausikaa.[16]

Yet there are serious difficulties. Nothing in the text of the *Odyssey* indicates that the Cyclopes lived in Sicily or, in fact, on an island at all. Phaiakian Scheria does seem to be an island, far out in the sea with no land near. Corfu is an island, but lies so close off the mainland that from the open sea, whence Odysseus approached it, and even from some places on the landward side, it is impossible to tell where the mainland ends and the island begins, or even that Corfu is an island at all. Yet as Odysseus first sees it (v.281).

> it looked like a shield lying on the misty face of the water.

External evidence raises still greater difficulties. The *Odyssey* substantially as we have it could not have been completed much before the end of the eighth century B.C. The traditional foundation dates for many Greek cities in the West are earlier than that. Sicilian Naxos is said to have been settled in 735 B.C., Syracuse and Korkyra in 734, and half a dozen others before 700; Kyme (Cumae), near Naples, claims even greater age. These dates are generally accepted by modern scholars, and the pottery in some places even goes back to Mycenaean times.[17] Thus, by the time of the *Odyssey*'s completion, the western Mediterranean as far as Sicily was not only well explored, but pretty well settled with Greek colonies, colonies almost or quite as Hellenic as their mother cities in old Greece. How could such a place belong simultaneously to the known world and the wonder world of the Wanderings? How could Korkyra be both itself and Scheria? Only, one might say, by embedding features conceived very early in the process of accumulation, and ignoring later phases.

This does not seem to be the normal process. Homer's Ithaka is Ithaka, not a wonderland. Sicily as Sikania is mentioned, as if it were a real place (xxiv.307); the land of the Sikels (presumably Sicilians) is a source or market for slaves, not Cyclopes or other

---

[15] See Baedeker's *Southern Italy* (1912), p. 410.
[16] See Baedeker's *Greece* (1909), p. 262.
[17] See J. Boardman, *The Greeks Overseas* (London, 1964), pp. 179–181.

monsters (xx.383; xxiv.211; 365; 389). Menelaos speaks of Libya among other far but real places, iv.83-85:

> I wandered to Cyprus and Phoenicia, to the Egyptians,
> I reached the Aithiopians, Eremboi, Sidonians,
> and Libya.

The place is preternaturally prosperous, but it keeps company with Cyprus, Phoenicia, Egypt, and Ethiopia, not with the Lotus-Eaters, and a relatively workaday Phoenician ship was carrying Odysseus there to be sold as a slave (xiv.295-297).

Those who would find true points of reference for Aiolos, the Phaiakians, Laistrygones, and the rest frequently offer the support of topographical detail from the Homeric text. Sometimes this is too general for identification, but often it is plausible. The little island off the land of the Cyclopes is described in thoughtful detail, as if seen by the eye of a prospective settler (ix.116-169); but where is it? The land of the Laistrygones is vividly presented; we can still ask the same question. In these and other cases, the descriptions may well be based on authentic reports from mariners.

But they also may be put in the wrong place. That is, to say it another way, for this is important, it is possible to combine topographical accuracy with geographical incoherence.

This seems actually to have happened in the case of Ithaka. Topographical details are scattered through the poem. The scholar can review these and honestly say that Homer seems to know his Ithaka, and what it is like.[18] Only he does not seem to know where it is. Listen to Odysseus himself, who *ought* to know, ix.21-26:

> I am at home in sunny Ithaka. There is a mountain
> there that stands tall, leaf-trembling Neritos, and there are islands
> settled around it, lying one very close to another.
> There is Doulichion and Same, wooded Zakynthos,
> but my island lies low and away, last of all on the water
> toward the dark, with the rest below facing east and sunshine.

This simply will not do for Ithaka (Thiaki), though that has the landmarks, for it lies tucked close in against the *eastern* side of the far larger Kephallenia (Same?). Homer's description would in fact

---

[18] See the chapter by F. H. Stubbings, in Wace and Stubbings, *Companion to Homer* (London and New York, 1962), pp. 398-421.

better suit Corfu (Korkyra), which all the world has already identified with Phaiakian Scheria.

I am thus forced back to the belief that the places of the Wanderings are combinations. They are made by the imagination. They
are in part sheer fancy; and sailors' stories can involve monsters
and enchanted places, as well as authentic report. But they probably contain bits and pieces of solid unassimilated fact. The lands
of the Wanderings seem to stand on the same footing as their inhabitants. These too are of this world and stature, rather than that
of Olympos and the Olympians. Yet they are not quite of this
world either. They are people endowed like no people we shall
ever meet, and live in places where no one, since Odysseus, will
ever go.[19] And thus the Land of the Dead, where Odysseus and his
men (so soon to die) are the only living visitors, takes its natural
place among the Wanderings. For it is described not as an underworld but as a far shore, with landmarks borrowed (perhaps) from
some or several true places in the real world.

If the *Odyssey* is a work of the imagination, then, we must ask,
are the Wanderings symbolic or allegorical? Do they represent the
story not of a man but of Man? Many have thought so.[20] I think
not. But the Wanderings do lend themselves to a morality, for it is
easy to read the adventures as a series of trials. The Greek authors
liked to dramatize the test (*peira*) by which a person established
his quality. Odysseus passes or at least survives the trials by terror
and force: the Kikonians, the Cyclops, the Laistrygones, the con-
frontation with the ghosts, Skylla, Charybdis, Zeus's storm,
Poseidon's storm. And there is trial by temptation. His men fail
disastrously against curiosity and hunger with the Bag of Winds
and the Cattle of the Sun, but Odysseus endures, and he endures
also against the temptations to stay with comfort and beauty and
give up the hard voyage home: the charms of the Lotus-Eaters,
Circe, the Sirens, Kalypso, Nausikaa.

But symbolism and allegory seem foreign to the biology of early
Greek epic; it is hard for me to think that the moral proposition

---

[19] "You will find where Odysseus wandered," said the Alexandrian geogra-
pher Eratosthenes, "when you find the cobbler who stitched the bag of the
winds." See Strabo, *Geography* i.2.15.

[20] For a recent statement and defense of this view, see G. deF. Lord,
Homeric Renaissance (New Haven, 1956).

came first, with the story shaped to present it. Even in the case of
Circe turning the men to swine, it is probably mistaken to read
anything more meaningful than a fairy-tale transformation. There
is plenty of morality in the *Odyssey*, but it is where it ought to be,
inextricably implicit in the story itself. This is a brilliant series of
adventures linked and fused by character. The tests (including the
tests on Ithaka) are passed by the exercise of virtues, viz. (in
ascending order) physical courage and strength; ingenuity where
these might fail; restraint, patience, tact, and self-control; and the
will for home.

These are the virtues not of Man, but of a particular valiant,
resourceful, much-enduring hero, established as such in the *Iliad*,
and developed in a development of the *Nostoi*, the sequel to the
Iliad.

Odysseus on Ithaka

In the middle of a line, xiii.187, we leave the Phaiakians forever,
without even learning what finally happened to them, and henceforth we are concerned almost exclusively with Odysseus on
Ithaka. He will not attack the suitors until Book xxii, and he will
not reveal himself to Penelope until Book xxiii. Thus the length
allotted to Odysseus on Ithaka is extraordinary. Nearly nine books,
more than twice the text given to the Great Wanderings, are devoted to the time from Odysseus's arrival to his dropping of disguise and attack on the suitors, and for nearly nine books very
little happens.

We can only guess at the purpose of this drawing-out. We may
observe some of the effects. The revelations and recognitions, by
Telemachos, Eumaios and Philoitios, Penelope, Laertes, are strung
out bit by bit. We are teased by the abortive recognitions by Argos
and Eurykleia, and by the times when the careful hero nearly
gives himself and the game away (xviii.90–94; xx.28–30). There is
the constant threat that Penelope will, at the very last moment,
give in to the suitors (xix.524–534; 576–581; xxi.68–79). There
arises that special irony where the audience or reader, in on the
whole secret, can watch the victims being gulled by the hero, his
merciless guarding divinity, and his equally merciless son.

The story of near-recognition is beautifully played out in the interview between the hero and his wife, where she confides in the stranger to whom she is so drawn that she can hardly let him go (xix.509). Here and elsewhere, the leisurely composition, in which talk is overwhelmingly predominant, gives opportunity to elaborate the characters. The epithets of the three leading persons—resourceful Odysseus, thoughtful Telemachos, and circumspect Penelope— gain depth and intensity through these slow books. Penelope, in particular, is done with great subtlety. Desperately pressed, with no power but her wits, charm, and heart, she plays a waiting game and never commits herself.

The leading suitors, Antinoös, Eurymachos, and Amphinomos, also gain some dimension. Both as a group and as individuals, in a few cases, the suitors could have been much simpler than they are. For the poet seems mostly to have seen the moral issue as just right against wrong.[21] The sin of the faithless maids and of the one faithless thrall is disloyalty. The sin of the suitors is perhaps this, too, but they also abuse hospitality. To Homer, perhaps because he was a wandering poet, this virtue is thematic, and again and again we are given object lessons on the right dealings between host and guest, through the conduct of Telemachos, Nestor and his family, Menelaos and a reformed Helen, the Phaiakians, Odysseus, Kalypso, Penelope. Horrid counter-examples are furnished by Polyphemos and the Laistrygones. The suitors are aware of the principle (xvii.481–487) but in action they are a living travesty of all proper custom. Thus they lose all divine favor. Not even an Olympian god is so prejudiced as to take their part.

Yet they are no indiscriminate group of villains, nor are they all villains. They are said to be plotting the murder of Telemachos but, once he has slipped past them, they seem irresolute about it (xvi. 371–406). They appear to be more an intolerable nuisance than an actual menace. They have some moral notions and some sense of decency (xvi.400–406; xvii.365–368; 481–487). While indirectly offending the gods by their treatment of people, they respect the gods and regularly observe the forms of religion. This, and their occasional kindnesses, do them no good (xvii.363–364). Odysseus tries to warn the best of them, but Athene has no mercy (xviii. 124–157).

Their doom seems excessive to me. I do not know how it seemed

---

[21] See, for one instance out of many, xxii.413–416.

to Homer. But Penelope cried over her pet geese (xix.535–558),
and Homer may have conceived some liking for his own creatures,
and put off, as long as he could, their necessary slaughter.

The End of the Odyssey

After the killing of the suitors and the reunion of Penelope and
Odysseus, the end of the *Odyssey* reads like a hurried composition.
The purpose of the second visit to the dead is not altogether clear.
It does, however, in some sense dispose of the suitors, whose bodies
were for some time lying about the palace (they are finally buried,
xxiv.417); and it does link the Ithakan episode with the background of the Trojan War, in a manner not uncongenial to the poet
of the eleventh book, if this is he.

On the other hand, the previous narrative demands a reunion
with Laertes, and it certainly demands some kind of patch-up of
the chaotic situation in Ithaka, where "all the best young men"
(i.245) are lying dead. A reconciliation is scrambled together by a
hasty and inadequate *deus ex machina,* which ends the epic. The
hand has lost its firmness,[22] but who can say for sure that the hand
is not Homer's?

The Odyssey and the Iliad

This brings us to the question of unity, which cannot be solved
but must be faced. For the *Odyssey,* as previously for the *Iliad,* I
have been writing as if on the assumption of a single master hand
or, in Kirk's phrase, monumental poet.[23] Only a study devoted to
disintegration would proceed otherwise. Such unity cannot be
proved, though the burden of proof is on the analysts rather than
on the unitarians. Such unity also, if it exists, is qualified by the
conditions of oral poetry, namely, the accumulation of saga material (less for the *Odyssey* than for the *Iliad*), and of formulaic
language.

If there was such a monumental poet for the *Odyssey,* and a

[22] See Page, *op. cit.,* pp. 101–130 and, in particular pp. 112–114.
[23] See, for instance, Kirk, *op. cit.,* p. 96.

monumental poet for the *Iliad*, were they the same man? I can only say as I have said before: that this cannot be proved; but that, if someone not Homer composed the *Odyssey*, nobody had a name to give him; and that the burden of proof rests on those who would establish separate authorship.

Still, it is well to note some of the similarities and differences in the two poems. The *Odyssey*, like the *Iliad*, ignores historical developments between the time of the originating events and the time of composition. In the *Odyssey*, as in the *Iliad*, this principle is violated by occasional slips, the so-called anachronisms. The *Odyssey* adds a few of its own: Sicilians, Phoenicians in the western seas, Dorians in Crete, consultation of oracles. Little can be proved by this. The important anachronisms are deeper and harder to assess. How far, for instance, does the picture of Ithaka reflect life in a Mycenaean palace, and how much does it reflect life in a baronial house of the poet's own day, centuries later?

The *Odyssey* seems later than the *Iliad* principally because it assumes the existence of the *Iliad*, or at least of a fully told tale of Troy. That does not mean it must be so much later that we require a separate author. It is a coherent sequel to the *Iliad* and does not contradict it.

Consider the characters who are carried over from one epic to the other. Judgment of characterization is admittedly a subjective business. For what my opinion is worth, I would say that Odysseus, Nestor, Agamemnon, Menelaos, Helen, and Achilleus are the same "people" in both poems.[24] Those qualities which mark the Odysseus of the *Odyssey*—strength and courage, ingenuity, patience and self-control—all characterize the same hero in the *Iliad*. His friendship with the Atreidae and Nestor, suggested in the *Iliad*, is still more notable in the *Odyssey*. And in the *Iliad* his determination to win the war matches his determination to win the homecoming in the *Odyssey*. To achieve both ends, he is ruthless. Nestor in his garrulity, Agamemnon in his self-pity, Menelaos in his courtesy and strong moral sense, Achilleus in his devotion to the ideal of the warrior, all repeat striking characteristics of the persons in the

---

[24] For a contrary view see, for instance, D. B. Monro, *Homer's Odyssey* (Oxford, 1901), vol. 2, pp. 290–291. Monro comments on the "marked falling-off in the character of the chief actor."

Iliad. And Helen is as self-centered as ever; in neither epic can she make a speech without talking about herself.

All this, if it is allowed, does not of course prove a single poet for the two poems. It could mean no more than that whoever composed the *Odyssey* knew his *Iliad* well. But here we come upon a striking fact. When the *Odyssey* recounts episodes from the tale of Troy, these episodes are never a part of the *Iliad* but seem to fall outside, either before or after, the action of the *Iliad*. Thus, apart from the Returns or *Nostoi,* we hear of the following:

> The Trojan Horse and the final battle for Troy, iv.271-289; viii.499-520; xi.523-537.
>
> Odysseus's spying expedition in Troy, iv.240-264 (rather than his spying expedition with Diomedes, *Iliad* X.254-578).
>
> His wrestling match with Philomeleïdes of Lesbos, iv.341-344 (rather than with Aias, *Iliad* XXIII.707-737).
>
> His fight in defense of the body of Achilleus, v.308-310 (rather than his fight alone against the Trojans when the other Achaians had fled, *Iliad* XI.401-488).
>
> The quarrel of Odysseus and Achilleus, viii.75-82 (rather than that of Agamemnon and Achilleus, *Iliad* I.1-305).
>
> The death and burial of Achilleus, xxiv.35-94 (rather than the death and burial of Patroklos).
>
> The quarrel of Odysseus and Aias over the armor of Achilleus, xi.541-564.
>
> The death of Antilochos, iv.187-188; 199-202.
>
> The exploits or excellences of heroes who reached Troy after the action of the *Iliad* was over, such as Neoptolemos, Eurypylos, and Memnon, xi.505-537, and Philoktetes, viii.219.
>
> The recruiting of the heroes, xxiv.114-119.

The exclusion of Iliadic episodes from the *Odyssey* can scarcely be accidental. We are left, as I see it, to choose between two conclusions. Either the poet of the *Odyssey* was ignorant of the *Iliad*;[25] or he deliberately avoided trespassing on the earlier poem. I cannot believe in the first alternative, and am forced to choose the second.

What are the other important *differences* between the two poems? Every Homeric scholar has his own list, and I must be

[25] This is the view of Page, *op. cit.,* pp. 158-159.

brief. To me, the main differences are details of the whole general style of narrative. The *Odyssey* concentrates on relatively small groups. Without nations embattled, the Olympians of the *Iliad* are less needed, and the first-person narrative of the Great Wanderings virtually excludes them. There are also a few important and well-known differences in the concept of the divinities. Hermes, more of a magician than Iris, takes over her functions as messenger. Aphrodite, not Charis, is the wife of Hephaistos. Olympos turns into a never-never land (vi.41–47), strangely like the Elysian Field which is Menelaos' destination (iv.561–569), and well in accord with the *Odyssey*'s wander-world of monsters and fairyland people. Invention in the *Odyssey* extends to name making; a list of young Phaiakians shows a dozen and a half names, all meaning something to do with seamanship and shipbuilding (viii.111–115). The little thumbnail sketches of slaughtered warriors in the *Iliad* have a more traditional sound; such sketches are rare in the *Odyssey*, where we do not deal in large masses. The poet of the *Iliad* shows much lyric imagination in his similes. The *Odyssey* is far poorer here, and much of the same material is used differently. Storms in the *Iliad* are used imaginatively in similes; there is no weather in the *Iliad*.[26] Storms in the *Odyssey* are something Odysseus must contend with. The humble workingman enters the *Iliad* only through simile, but in the *Odyssey* he is there in the flesh.

When we come to language, rhythm, metrical phrasing, the overmastering impression is one of unity. If there were two (or more) poets, they were trained in the same tradition of formula. Agamemnon is hailed in the *Iliad* (II.434, etc.) as

Son of Atreus, most lordly and king of men, Agamemnon,

and so he is in the *Odyssey* when the occasion arises (xi.397). His answering address (xi.405),

Son of Laertes and seed of Zeus, resourceful Odysseus,

is common to both epics. So is the summons to assembly (*Iliad* II. 50–52; *Odyssey* ii.6–8), the introduction of a speaker (*Iliad* I.73, etc.; *Odyssey* ii.160, etc.), the course of ships through the water (*Iliad* I.481–483; *Odyssey* ii.427–429). In both epics, children are

[26] Contrast the story told by Odysseus to Eumaios about warriors on night picket duty before Troy, xiv.462–502. The chilliness of the task is emphasized.

innocent, women are deep-girdled, iron is gray, ships are hollow, words are winged and go through the barrier of the teeth, the sea is wine-blue, barren, and salt, bronze is sharp and pitiless. The list is almost endless. Even the Ithakans are strong-greaved Achaians (*Odyssey* ii.72; xx.146), though they are not armed.

The *Odyssey* has many phrases, journey formulae for instance, which are not found in the *Iliad.*[27] Naturally, the *Iliad* has many combat formulae which are missing from the *Odyssey*. But when combat finally ensues between Odysseus and the suitors, the poet repeats brief formulae and even sizable sequences (compare *Iliad* XV.479–481 and *Odyssey* xxii.122–124). Adaptation may be necessary. Amphinomos goes down, *Odyssey* xxii.94:

> He fell, thunderously, and took the earth full on his forehead.

We cannot quite have the standard *Iliad* line:

> He fell, thunderously, and his armor clattered upon him.

Amphinomos has no armor. Occasionally, a few lines from a combat in the *Iliad* can fit a context in the *Odyssey* which is not military. The language for the Cyclops' throwing a stone is the same as that used for Aias (*Iliad* VII.268–269; *Odyssey* ix.537–538). The death of Odysseus's steersman (xii.412–414) is neatly adapted from the death of Epikles on the wall (*Iliad* XII.384–386).

Can the formula in a changed setting ever mean parody? Sarpedon advances on the wall of the Achaians like a lion against a guarded sheepfold (*Iliad* XII.299–301), and that is appropriate; but the same language is adapted to Odysseus's embarrassed advance on a group of frightened girls (*Odyssey* vi.130; 133–134). When Telemachos sneezes, the sneeze "clashed horribly" *Odyssey* xvii.542); the phrase was used of the helmet of Hektor in battle (*Iliad* XV.648) and other warlike noises. Eumaios is called *orchamos andron,* "leader of men" (xiv.121). This could mean "foreman (of swineherds)," which is what he is, but it suggests "commander of armies," which is what it means in the *Iliad.* It has been suggested that the arrangement that "noble swineherd" made for his sows reflected those made by Priam for his daughters (*Odyssey* xiv.13–15; *Iliad* VI.244–246). There are other such combinations which, with enough good will, can be seen as paro-

---

[27] On this subject see Kirk, *op. cit.,* pp. 293–297.

dies. It is hard to be sure, but such amusements with formula would be in accord with the generally lighter tone of the *Odyssey*.[28]

Yet these very manipulations of metrical phrases attest a deep, intimate similarity of ear and verse building which can only be suggested here. We can illustrate by a short phrase taken almost at random: *peri chroï*, which means "next the skin" or "around the body," and having the metrical scheme ∪–∪ ∪. It is used in a dozen *otherwise quite different* lines in the two poems. But it always comes in exactly the same place in the line, to form the line-end *peri chroï*–∪∪– –. This shows not merely the reuse of materials, but a constant habit of metrical thought.

There is much that is obscure about the functions of a monumental poet. Within the limits of my ignorance, I can think of one Homer, composing, or completing, first the *Iliad*, then the *Odyssey*. Or I can think of an old master, called *Homer*, mainly responsible for the *Iliad*; and a young master, favored apprentice and poetic heir; perhaps a nephew or son-in-law; also going by the name, or assuming the name, of Homer; and mainly responsible for the *Odyssey*. I find the second combination more persuasive, but that is all I can say for it.

---

[28] The words of Hektor to Andromache, *Iliad* VI.490–493 are repeated twice in the *Odyssey* (i.356–359; xxi. 350–353), and the last line and a half at xi.352–353; but the "fighting" of the *Iliad* passage is changed each time.

Initiatory Motifs
in the Story of Telemachus

by Charles W. Eckert

Critics of the *Odyssey*, from the Scholiast to Werner Jaeger, have frequently commented on the "educational" nature of Telemachus's voyage to Pylos and Sparta and the transformation from boy to man that occurs during the trip.[1] The indecisive and mother-bound youth of the first books returns filled with the *menos* of the Homeric hero and joins in the cleansing of the house of Odysseus, more as his father's peer than as his son. Seen in this light, the story of Telemachus has a developed plot of its own and could be excerpted, if one chose, to form a separate work.

This common critical view has given direct support to the combined textual-critical arguments for the existence of a *Telemachia*, an independent poem which was wedded to a Voyage and Return of Odysseus to form the present *Odyssey*. The history of this argument is bound up with the almost two-hundred-year-old debate between the "unitarians" and the ["Analysts"] and may be traced through a vast bibliography.[2] But whether or not the *Telemachia* was once a separate work, it is substantially independent from the adventures of Odysseus and has always invited criticism in its own right.

From *The Classical Journal* 59 (1963), 49–57. Copyright © 1963 by the Classical Association of the Middle West and South, Inc. Reprinted by permission of the publisher and the estate of Charles W. Eckert, George B. Van Arsdale, Literary Executor.

[1] *Paideia: the ideals of Greek culture,* 2d ed. (New York 1939), 1. 29–34. Jaeger's notes contain further bibliography on the subject of Telemachus' "education."

[2] A selective bibliography with a discussion is given by Denys Page, *The Homeric Odyssey* (Oxford 1955), pp. 73–81. Of special importance is his Appendix on critical issues involved in discussions of the *Telemachia* (165–82).

To call the *Telemachia* the story of a young prince's education, however, is to define it somewhat imprecisely; the kind of education Telemachus undergoes is that known throughout the ancient world and modern primitive societies as *initiation*. The importance of rites of social initiation for Greek society has been frequently emphasized, notably by Jane Harrison (*Themis*, Cambridge 1912), Henri Jeanmaire (*Couroi et Courètes*, Lille 1939), George Thomson (*Aeschylus and Athens*, London 1941), and by most modern students of the Eleusiniana. Partly because of the prominence of initiation rites in the popular mystery cults, initiatory symbolism enters Platonic and Neoplatonic philosophy, alchemy, and mystical disciplines of many forms, and many initiatory rites or paradigms are employed in religion and literature until Renaissance times.

The real extent of the popularity of initiatory symbolism and the probable reasons for this popularity have not been sufficiently studied. The usual assumption made by students of religion and literature is that any group of initiatory motifs must be a "survival" from earlier social rituals practised in that particular society. The Cambridge school of myth-ritual study, under the influence of nineteenth-century theories of "cultural evolution," gave popularity to the belief that the resemblances between advanced religions and myths and primitive ritual (largely documented in modern societies) were to be explained genetically: prehistoric ritual must have given rise to the historical forms. There are several dangers in assuming this: first we cannot be certain that prehistoric rituals were the same as those documented among modern primitives; second, it is possible that initiatory symbolism arises psychogenetically or is borrowed from neighboring cultures; and third, the concentration upon hypothetical primitive sources takes our attention away from the advanced meanings which may be expressed through initiatory symbolism in higher cultures. Initiation is one of the constants of human society, not merely as a social ritual, but also as a symbolic system capable of expressing transition or transcendence from any polar state to its opposite. Just as initiation appears in social ritual wherever rites are employed to effect the transition from boy to man, so initiation as a symbolic system is employed universally to express such transcendental movements as ignorance to knowledge, secularity to sacrality, or life to death or immortality.

Whatever the importance of rituals of social initiation in the pre-

historic Near East, the initiatory symbolisms found in historical
religions and literatures must exist because of a *need* for this sort
of symbolism and not merely as a survival of primitive social forms.
Such a need existed, I believe, for Homer: the initiatory paradigm
upon which the story of Telemachus is built gives the most apt
symbolism for expressing the movement from boy to man which is
at the heart of the *Telemachia.* This is, however, but one of a
constellation of meanings which Homer derives from the paradigm;
and many of these meanings are not prominent in primitive initiation ritual, as I shall attempt to demonstrate. The important point
to be made at present is that the initiatory paradigm employed by
Homer is probably not derived directly from ritual and cannot be
adequately analyzed in terms of ritual analogues. In order to sub-
stantiate this statement I shall first give a brief description of
initiation as a social ritual, then examine the initiatory elements in
the *Telemachia* in detail, and finally examine the particular meanings Homer seems to derive from the initiatory paradigm.

Initiation rituals, usually called "puberty rituals" by ethnogra-
phers, are as widespread as rites concerned with crops or such
major events as birth and death. The rites usually include killing an
enemy or performing a sacrifice, or both; removal from the group
to a hut, sacred ground, or unfrequented area; the endurance of
ordeals and the performance of feats; instruction in the group
myths, which include knowledge of origins, morality, the nature
of deity, etc.; some rite of "marking" such as circumcision or
scarification; and finally, investment with adult objects or clothing
and a return to the group. The entire experience is extremely
threatening because of the presence of the gods who usually "consume" or "kill" the initiates at some point in the rites so that they
may return as those "reborn" to a higher status. The central symbolism of death and rebirth is well understood and is often ingen-
iously elaborated. Boys are frequently removed secretly and at
night, and the mothers are told that the gods have stolen them and
may kill them. This helps effect a break with the maternal world,
since the boys' "death" is to a large degree a death to childhood
and effeminizing influence. It is also, as Mircea Eliade has shown
at length,[3] a death to the secular condition and to ignorance. The

[3] *Birth and rebirth,* tr. Willard Trask (New York 1958). This is the best
general study of both primitive and advanced religious initiation and contains
a full bibliography.

central rites of instruction give the boys the knowledge of the myths, moral codes and rituals—a knowledge which defines man in his religious and social roles and makes him a complete and responsible adult.

That such rituals were known to the Greeks in pre-Homeric times is highly probable, even if one argues only from the grounds that the vast majority of primitive societies employ initiation rites. This probability is increased by the fact that the Eleusiniana, the most popular cult of classical times, exhibits a clear initiatory structure: such rites as ablution and sacrifice, the journey from Athens to the sacred ground of the Telesterion at Eleusis in the company of a *mystagogos*, and the final *epopteia* or revelation of the sacred all have their analogues in social initiation. Greek education and the rearing of young men in general also recall initiatory practices at many points, especially in Sparta. But when we move from the social and religious spheres to those of myth and epic we move into a different dimension—one as large as the Near East itself, from which the early literature of the Greeks derives. It now seems an inescapable conclusion that the plot structures founded on the heroic quest, acts of purgation and regeneration, the slaying of chthonic demons, and the expiation of bloodguilt are rooted in the sacred myths of the Near East and are disseminated and transformed by singers. To look in each society for a specific ritual which may have given rise to a myth known to that society is to ignore the cosmopolitan and itinerant nature of recited story.

Albert Lord, who has studied at length the techniques of modern Yugoslavian epic singers, notes that stories are transmitted as complexes of motifs rather than as memorized texts (this is not true, of course, if a particular text has been fixed in writing and is considered inviolable).[4] The motif is merely an act or situation—a murder, or marriage, or imprisonment—and the complex of motifs which makes up a "plot" may be all that is kept intact as a story is transmitted from region to region or transferred from hero to hero. Motifs may be variously rationalized, reordered, or dropped from the complex in favor of something more intelligible to the particular singer and his audience.

The initiatory paradigm at the heart of the *Telemachia* appears to be such a complex: it does not, of course, include all of Telema-

[4] *The singer of tales* (Cambridge, Mass. 1960), pp. 68–98.

chus's activities; but it does include most of his important and many of his most puzzling actions. As stated before, initiation often begins with a nocturnal theft of the young boys by the older men (usually dressed as mythic beings) and the removal of the boys to a secluded place. Telemachus's voyage, undertaken at night and without Penelope's knowledge, is made in the company of Athena who, in the guise of Mentor ('teacher'), directs his initiation. The sacred ground to which the initiates proceed for the most critical of the rites may be a permanent sacred area, such as the Telesterion at Eleusis, or it may be an area especially marked out for the occasion.[5] Rites conducted on this sacred ground are believed to reactualize mythic events and mythic time (the time when the events were first performed), and the performers become the gods or demigods involved in these events.[6] For Telemachus, this sacred ground is the lower Peloponnese, the ancient home of Mycenaean civilization, inhabited by two heroes of the Trojan War, Nestor and Menelaus. It is to Pylos and Sparta, far from his home, his mother, and all childhood associations, that Telemachus must go in order to receive the knowledge without which he cannot become a man.

During the second phase initiates usually endure periods of seclusion in a dark and threatening place and live in imminent fear of being destroyed by the gods. As Eliade states, "a considerable number of initiation rites reactualize the motif of death in darkness and at the hands of Divine Beings."[7] The psychological function of this is obvious, but its symbolic function, its implications of death for the boy and rebirth into a world of men, must be emphasized. The instruction that occurs during this phase is little more than a retelling of the myths which contain the knowledge without which one is not a man: the creation of the world and of the

[5] The concept of "sacred space" is universal in primitive religious thought and has been extensively surveyed by Mircea Eliade, *The sacred and the profane,* tr. Willard Trask (New York 1959).

[6] The assumption of legendary roles by the officiators in primitive and ancient religious ceremonies is a universal custom. The role of hierophant at Eleusis was filled by members of the Eumolpidae, "descendants" of the mythical Eumolpus, the shepherd-god who brought the mysteries to Eleusis in the reign of Erechtheus; and Plutarch said that in his own day it was "Eumolpus" who initiated the Hellenes (*De exilio* 607B).

[7] *Birth and rebirth,* p. 9.

group, the early struggles of the divine founders with primal forces, and stories which embody the practical morality of the group usually make up the bulk of this "knowledge." The motifs of death in darkness and instruction are both prominent in the *Telemachia.* The threat of death comes, of course, from the suitors, who recognize that Telemachus has begun to mature and who determine to kill him upon his return by waylaying his ship; and both the voyages to and from Pylos are dangerous night voyages made under the close supervision of a supernatural being, Athena. The instruction that Telemachus receives is a recounting by Nestor and Menelaus of the most critical myth of his society, the story of the Trojan War and its aftermath. The fact that the Trojan War is for Nestor and Menelaus a matter of recent history does not diminish its importance as a source of heroic "knowledge," and I shall consider later the great significance of the Trojan story for Telemachus's personal development.

The third phase, which sometimes takes place on or near the sacred ground, sometimes at the place of seclusion, is that of physical initiation. Whatever rite is performed, whether it is as harsh and dangerous as subincision or merely scarification or piercing the septum of the ear, the alteration is less specifically sexual than it is the creation of an unalterable and conspicuous mark of adult male status. This phase is continuous with the fourth, which is often accompanied by the revelation of certain sacral objects and by long trips which retrace routes originally blazed by the mythical beings (as in the journey from Athens to Eleusis made by the Eleusinian initiates). Sometimes all four stages are passed while the men and boys travel an extensive, difficult route. Finally, the return of the initiates to the entire group often involves a mock rejection of the mother or a mock or real tyrannizing of women in general, a practice that may also occur earlier in the ceremony. In the *Odyssey,* the final battle in the hall fuses most of these motifs, including the scarification of Telemachus, the revelation (*epopteia*) of the totemic aegis of Athena to all present, and a real tyrannizing of women (the hanging of the twelve maidservants) by Telemachus. In both the generalized ritual and the *Telemachia* the essential symbolisms of travel, danger, instruction, physical alteration, the tyrannizing of women, and death and rebirth are readily apparent.

At this point it may be objected that some of the motifs, particularly the *epopteia* and the tyrannizing of women, are no part of the traditional *Telemachia* and might as well pertain to Odysseus. With this I am in full agreement: as has been frequently noted, the voyage of Odysseus includes many motifs found in initiatory myths and rituals.[8] It is not so "pure" an initiatory structure as is the voyage of Telemachus, but in Odysseus and Telemachus we do have a "doubled" father-son hero resembling those common in Near Eastern myth, and some of the final initiatory motifs may at one time have pertained to both heroes.

With this generalized pattern in mind, we may now look more closely at the activities of the major figures in the *Telemachia*. The first scene of the *Odyssey*, which pictures Zeus musing on the folly of Aegisthus whom Orestes was bound to slay as soon as he achieved manhood, becomes immediately significant for Telemachus when Athena announces her intention of going to Ithaca to counsel him to visit Pylos and Sparta. The real purpose of this visit, she states, is that he may earn repute among men and show that he is ready to put aside childishness and establish his authority with the suitors and his mother (1.271–302). Athena's true role in the *Telemachia,* of course, is that of a Kourotrophos—a term that in most modern commentaries is translated as "child-bearer" or "child-nurturer." Harrison and Nilsson,[9] however, have shown that *kouros* had the preclassical meaning of "young man just come to maturity," a definition which applies to the over 190 known examples of the kouros-type statue. As the Mentor to an initiate, Athena clearly resembles the *mystagogos* of the Eleusiniana and the older men of more primitive ritual.

With Athena's first visit concluded, Telemachus immediately begins his transformation by speaking sternly to his mother and to the suitors, calling forth the comment by Antinous that he has changed and that the gods must be helping him (1.384–7). The transformation continues during the great debate in Book 2, in which Telemachus tells the suitors of his plans and advises them that he will return to end their spoiling of his father's house now that he is "grown." Meanwhile, Athena (in the temporary guise of

[8] See particularly Gabriel Germain, *Genèse de l'Odyssée* (Paris 1954), pp. 78–86, 126–8, 131–2.

[9] *Themis* (Cambridge 1912), pp. 11–12; and *The Minoan-Mycenaean religion and its survivals in Greek religion,* 2d ed. (Lund 1950), p. 547, respectively.

Telemachus) has secured a ship and a crew of twenty young men. When provisions have been taken aboard and night has fallen, the perilous trip begins. The combined motifs of darkness and enclosure in a womblike space (the ship) with a mythic being or beings in attendance are constants in initiatory rituals and myths.[10] Jung has studied these motifs in many initiatory plots and has noted that the sea journey by night is a critical and decisive event in which the emphasis is not upon the "eternal recurrence" of the trip, but rather upon a "transformation into something higher."[11] No interpretation could be more appropriate to the journey Telemachus makes.

Upon their arrival in Pylos, Athena reassures the still timid Telemachus that his heart will prompt him to speak correctly in the presence of Nestor, and he approaches the legendary hero, encountering first Nestor's son Peisistratus who henceforth remains his companion during his stay in Pylos and Sparta.[12] The details of Telemachus's conversations with the aged Nestor need not be recounted. Considered broadly, the conversations achieve the same two purposes as those held later with Menelaus in Sparta: they display the growing confidence and rhetorical ability of Telemachus and they transmit to him the "knowledge" without which he cannot be a complete man—the history of the Trojan War and the ensuing catastrophes that befell the Greeks. These myths free Telemachus from his childish past by establishing a new role for him in a higher reality. One remembers Telemachus's words to Antinous before leaving Ithaca: "I am old enough to learn from others what has happened and to feel my own strength at last" (2.314–5). The equation knowledge = strength seems implicit here. The story of Orestes is referred to by both Nestor and Menelaus, who underline its monitory significance for Telemachus and establish it as the particular segment of the "matter" of Troy which *defines* Telemachus in his new role as an adult. Now that the pattern of conduct is clear, Telemachus can act.

---

[10] Eliade, *Birth and rebirth*, pp. 51–60.

[11] Jolande Jacobi, *Complex, archetype, symbol in the psychology of C. G. Jung* (New York 1959), p. 186.

[12] Peisistratus resembles companions found in other initiatory myths (Orestes–Pylades; Heracles–Alcon; Theseus–Pirithous). Young men already initiated frequently accompany boys undergoing initiation.

With the most important stage of his initiation concluded, Telemachus returns to Ithaca, again by night and under threat of death at the hands of the suitors. The long scenes in the hut of Eumaeus, where father and son are reunited, have no specific counterparts in initiation ritual, though they do reveal Telemachus's new maturity by demonstrating his resolute desire to prove his courage against the suitors and his ability to debate the plan of attack with so experienced a warrior as his father.

Perhaps the most interesting initiatory details, however, are found immediately before and during the final battle itself. A great deal has been written about the scene in which Athena leads Telemachus and Odysseus into the hall on the eve of battle in order to hide away the arms kept there (19.1–40). Athena precedes the two warriors bearing a golden lamp that sheds upon the walls and beams and pillars a blazing light and makes Telemachus exclaim at such a "great marvel." Pfeiffer has recently argued for a cultic significance in this scene.[13] In terms of initiation, however, the scene recalls nothing so much as the reports of the final ceremonies inside the Telesterion at Eleusis which speak of the blaze of light that illuminates the hall when the initiates enter for the final rites.

With the hall prepared for battle, Odysseus waits for the sign from Zeus that will let him know that the gods favor his enterprise and will aid him. When the sign comes, the general battle begins; but it is soon interrupted by an extensive debate between Odysseus and the suitors and by the struggle in the storeroom between Melanthius, Philoetius and Eumaeus. Athena then sheds her guise of Mentor, assumes her most common and ancient epiphany, that of a bird, and flies to a roof beam from which she may survey the battle (22.239–40). Taking complete control, she directs the spears in their flights and tries the skill and courage of both heroes by withholding the strength they need to complete the slaughter. Then two curious things happen. First, Athena permits a spear thrown by Amphimedon to cut Telemachus near the wrist.[14] Immediately thereafter Athena lifts on high her "man-destroying" (*phthisim-*

---

[13] R. Pfeiffer, "Die goldene Lampe der Athene," *Studi italiani di filologia classica* 28 (1956) 426–33.

[14] Another spear wounds Eumaeus, but this fact does not alter the significance of what happens to Telemachus. Homer is not creating an initiatory plot; he is rationalizing one and in the process undoubtedly making additions of his own.

broton) aegis, throwing the suitors into a panic and sending them fleeing like kine.[15] Within the space of a dozen lines all but a few of the suitors are dead or dying. The motifs of scarification and the *epopteia* of the sacred symbol of the goddess all but complete the "rites" through which Telemachus has been transformed from a womanish boy to an heroic slayer of men. His final act is the hanging of the twelve maidens who had kept company with the suitors. This tyrannizing of women is a motif commonly found in European initiation scenarios, and is usually the direct consequence of the hero's acquisition of the *menos* or *ferg*—the overabundant heroic "furor" and strength—that the initiation rites have instilled in him and that must be burned out, so to speak, before he can return to normal society.[16] It also, of course, establishes his transcendence of the feminine ties of youth by displaying his absolute mastery over women.

The greatest danger in drawing parallels, as I have done, is that the validity of the argument may be thought to hinge upon the acceptability of all the detailed analogues suggested rather than upon the cumulative "proof" provided by the entire discussion. It is also important to note that Homer's use of an initiatory paradigm is in no way unique, but is rather very much *au courant,* not simply with respect to Greek social custom and religious ritual, but with respect to the Near Eastern literature of his era. If Greek myth did not come to us in such fragmented form, other examples of initiatory plots might be adduced: for instance, any composite version of the myths of Heracles, Theseus, Orestes, Erechtheus, or the Cretan Dionysus, to mention the best known, abounds with initiatory motifs. But the lack of a complete early text for any of these myths makes it impossible to say whether they at one time contained coherent initiatory patterns like that found in the

---

[15] The revelation of sacral objects in initiatory rites is an event of such importance that it is fraught with danger even for the initiates. Its effects upon the uninitiated, should they accidentally observe the ceremonies, is universally regarded as disastrous. The terror of the suitors upon seeing the aegis of Athena is due to the sacral potency of the aegis, not to the mere presence of the goddess. In sculpture and art Athena's aegis is depicted with a gorgon's head in its center and a fringe of writhing serpents—as if to emphasize its fearful totemic power.

[16] For an excellent discussion of this concept in European myth see Georges Dumézil, *Horace et les Curiaces* (Saint-Amand 1942), pp. 11–33.

Telemachia. The Hebrews, however, preserved more complete versions of their heroic stories, and very coherent initiatory patterns may be discovered in the stories of Moses, of the Exodus itself (a group initiation),[17] and of Jacob, Samson and David. The story of Moses, in particular, exhibits an almost pure initiatory structure and includes all the acts normally performed during social initiations. The priestly redactors of this story have transformed and rationalized some of the motifs, but on the whole they have preserved the pattern of initiation itself and have simply made it significant at the level of sacred history by reducing Moses to an instrument of deity whose "initiation" attunes him to divine purpose instead of infusing him with autochthonous power.

The great value of the initiatory paradigm, as I have noted earlier, is that it can express a number of symbolisms equally well. The symbolism Homer derives from it can best be understood in the perspective of the shift from "myth to history" which Eric Voegelin and Mircea Eliade have sketched in broad outline and which occurred almost simultaneously in Greece and Israel.[18] Earlier Near Eastern societies in their religious rituals and myths displayed a desire to live in an "eternal present" and to abolish history through repetitions of the creation and cyclical symbolisms of many sorts; but the new sense of living in history demanded new symbolisms of transition, linear movement, and transcendence which were elaborated in a new group of symbolic orders.

Among these orders (following Voegelin) were Greek epic, philosophy and drama, and the Hebrew conception of historical revelation. Each in its way makes a radical break with myth at the same time that it retains much of the content and some of the characteristics of myth. The initiatory paradigm becomes popular in cult and literature during the centuries when this major shift is occurring. The reason for this, I believe, is that initiation is peculiarly apt for expressing symbolisms appropriate both to myth and to history: the death and rebirth and the voyage and return of the initiate are perfect vehicles for the expression of repetitive and cyclical movements, while the change from boy to man and from

[17] For initiatory motifs in the story of the Exodus see Theodor Reik, *Mystery on the mountain* (New York 1959).

[18] Voegelin, *Order and history,* vols. 1–2 (Baton Rouge 1956–7); Eliade, *The myth of the eternal return* (New York 1954).

ignorance to knowledge provide the potential for transitional and transcendental symbolisms. The range of meanings latent in initiation may be appreciated by comparing the myths of the initiations of Demophoon and Heracles (aetiological for the founding of the Greater and Lesser Eleusiniana, respectively), in which initiation is little more than a rite of toughening or cleansing, with the education of Telemachus, and with the figurative initiation of the philosopher in Plato's *Phaedrus*. Plato's use of initiatory terminology drawn from popular cult sets an example followed by Platonists and Neoplatonists until the Renaissance (especially Plotinus and Ficino), and if we view the *Telemachia* in the context of this entire tradition, the analogues from primitive ritual become less significant and the advanced symbolism latent in the initiatory paradigm more apparent.

Perhaps the most striking difference between the initiations of Telemachus and those of such mythic heroes as Heracles or Theseus is that Telemachus is pictured as fulfilling an ideal pattern of conduct created by an earlier hero, Orestes. Myth lacks any perspective of historical depth, since it always deals with those who first performed certain actions—with the creators, so to speak, of the paradigms of conduct. But Homer creates the kind of historical perspective that makes for typological thought. To what degree Homer's myth of Orestes was initiatory is impossible to say, but according to the traditions known to the tragedians, Orestes underwent some sort of initiation before purging the House of Atreus. In the company of a tutor he spent a number of years at the sacred center of Delphi, where he must have been instructed in the history of the House of Atreus and his duty to avenge his father's death. Shortly before his return, an urn filled with his "ashes" was exhibited to Aegisthus, recalling the motif of the "death" of the initiate which precedes his rebirth. After purification by Apollo, Orestes returned to kill Aegisthus and his mother in a scene that in the *Choephori* is deliberately assimilated to the final ceremonies of the Eleusiniana.[19] One should also note that the motifs of madness, self-mutilation, and extensive travel found in the *Oresteia* are commonplace in initiation scenarios.

If Homer knew the tradition containing all these specific analogues with their ritualistic overtones, he ignored most of it. The

[19] George Thomson, *Aeschylus and Athens* (London 1941), p. 270.

analogues he pursues are of a new order—the product of a shift from seeing traditional story as a sequence of acts to be understood in the context of ritual, to seeing the story as a general paradigm from which many meanings may be derived. Telemachus's voyage is not the ritualized fulfillment of a prophetic injunction, but a supervised quest for self-knowledge which reaches its goal in the realization that the House of Odysseus may become another House of Atreus unless he can imitate the courage and decisiveness of Orestes. This growth to maturity *through* paradigmatic knowledge, which is certainly the central symbolism of the *Telemachia,* differs from primitive instruction in the group myths by its emphasis upon the necessity for a personal decision on Telemachus's part. Knowledge is not given in an obligatory social rite; it must be sought, and, when found, accepted and converted into action. Telemachus's agon, compared to Orestes', is muted and distinctively human, yet its successful conclusion is the prelude to the reordering of the House of Odysseus and Telemachus's winning of *kleos* among men. His initiation, like those of Moses or David, has only its motif structure in common with the ritualized world of early myth. Homer has discovered a latent symbolism which accords with his historical perspective and has made "coming of age" an acquisition of the knowledge that makes for order and a discovery of the necessity for making decisions in a world which, as Zeus implies at the beginning of the *Odyssey,* is deterministic only for men who are weak of spirit. To this central symbolism Homer adds other conceptions not emphasized in primitive ritual, particularly Telemachus's growth in rhetorical ability and his associated mastery over the suitors, servants, and his mother upon his return.

The recognition that the *Telemachia* is founded upon an ordered paradigmatic structure should help answer those who have argued that the voyage of Telemachus is not substantive enough to stand as a separate work, or that the real purpose of the trip is to seek news of his father, or that the journey is an excuse to bring Nestor, Menelaus and Helen into the plot. Telemachus is both a major and an indispensable character, for upon his development, no less than upon the return of Odysseus, hinges the fate of Ithaca. One must remember that had not Odysseus nodded in warning, Telemachus would have strung the bow, and that he is ready to rule in Ithaca when Odysseus again leaves. Because Telemachus moves among the Herculean figures of Athena, Nestor, Menelaus and Orestes, his stature seems dwarfed and his agon of growth less dramatic than the sagas related to him by the reminiscing survivors of the battle of Troy. But in the *Telemachia* he is the hero, one whose human fears, youthful awkwardness and awe of the older heroes accentuates rather than detracts from the clear courage of his decision to confront the brutish suitors regardless of their numbers or strength. At the end of the *Odyssey* his shadow is as long as Orestes', not because it is also cast by the distant light from flaming Troy, but because he followed the advice to "think upon Orestes," and grew.

The Untypical Hero

by W. B. Stanford

There is nothing freakish about Odysseus's personality in the
Homeric poems. In the *Iliad* Homer endows him with the normal
qualities of an Achaean hero—princely birth, good physique,
strength, skill in athletics and battle, courage, energy, and eloquence.[1] But in most of these Odysseus is surpassed or equalled
by some of his colleagues at Troy. The Atreidae and Aeacids are of
more illustrious lineage. Agamemnon and Menelaus are of more impressive stature. Achilles and Ajax surpass him in strength and force

Reprinted from *The Ulysses Theme: A Study in the Adaptability of a
Traditional Hero,* 2d ed. (New York: Barnes and Noble, 1964), pp. 66–80.
Copyright © 1954 by Basil Blackwell, Oxford. Reprinted by permission of
the publisher, Basil Blackwell, and the author. Greek words in the notes have
been transcribed or translated, and notes emended, by permission of the
publisher and author.

[1] For studies of Odysseus's general characteristics in Homer see especially
Shewan, *The lay of Dolon* (London, 1911), chapter twenty (containing a survey of older views), Geddes, *The problem of the Homeric Poems* (London,
1878), (subject to Shewan's corrections), and Lang, *Homer and the Epic*
(London, 1893), chapter eight. Mure remarks elsewhere (*Critical History of
the Language and Literature of Ancient Greece,* 2d ed. [London, 1854] 1,
412) "like the fabulous Lycian sphinx, which combined the nature of the lion
and serpent with its own proper body of Chimaera, Ulysses, whether the king,
the beggar, the warrior, or the traveller, is still in word and deed Ulysses": cf.
Hole, *An essay on the character of Ulysses as delineated by Homer* (London,
1807), pp. 143–4: "the more minutely it (Ulysses' character) is examined,
the more evidently we find that the design, however bold, is exceeded by the
happiness of the execution."
   Since this was written I have seen two other notable discussions of Homer's
conception of Odysseus: Hubert Schrade, *Götter und Menschen Homers*
(Stuttgart, 1952), pp. 225–59, in which Odysseus is characterized as the first
uomo universale. a prototype in some respects of the Sophists, but differing
from them in his all-pervading piety; and E. Beaujon, *Acte et passion du
héros* (Geneva, 1948), in which some new symbolical interpretations of Odysseus are examined.

of arms. Diomedes is more gallant and dashing in battle. Even in oratory he is not unrivalled.

The fact is, of course, that Odysseus is not the chief hero of the *Iliad*. Achilles, and after him Ajax, Hector, Diomedes, and the Atreidae, are more prominent.[2] Not that the *Iliad* presents Odysseus as a minor hero: he has his triumphs in the council and in the assembly, on the field of battle and in the athletic contests. But his unique personality is not allowed to divert attention from the *Iliad*'s main themes, the wrath of Achilles and the death of Hector. On the other hand, in the *Odyssey* he, "the man of many turns," is the main theme, and his personal qualities become specifically luminous against the sordidness of his environment, as he makes his way among foolish shipmates, ruthless monsters, and greedy usurpers. Yet here, too, Odysseus meets his equals at times. Eumaeus the swineherd shows a loyalty and gentle courtesy quite as fine as his, and Penelope is wily enough to outwit him in their final recognition scene.

By endowing Odysseus with a share of the normal heroic qualities Homer avoided any suggestion that he was an eccentric figure or a narrowly limited type. But at the same time Homer, especially in the *Iliad*, skilfully succeeded in distinguishing Odysseus by slight deviations from the norm in almost every heroic feature. In his ancestry there was the unique Autolycan element. In physique he had the unusually short legs and long torso described by Antenor and Helen in *Il.* 3, 190 ff. He reminded Helen of a sturdy ram, she

---

[2] Odysseus admits inferiority in martial valour to Achilles (*Il.* 19, 217 ff.) while claiming superiority in intelligence, which he tactfully attributes to his greater age. (See additional note below.) The common soldiers rated Ajax, Diomedes and Agamemnon as fighters next to Achilles (*Il.* 7, 179–80). Hyginus, 114, gives inaccurate statistics of the "kills" of the Greek champions: Achilles leads with 72, followed by Teucer (30) and Ajax (28). Odysseus is second last with 12 to Menelaus's 8. Lang (*Anthropology and the classics*, [Oxford, 1908] pp. 60–61; cf. *World of Homer*, p. 250) holds that it "would not be hard to show that Odysseus is really the hero of the *Iliad*, as well as of the *Odyssey*, the man whom the poet admires most . . . " (one may admit the second view without agreeing with the first: a poet's hero is not necessarily the same as his poem's hero). Against this see also Jaeger, *Paideia* (Oxford, 1939), I, p. 7, where Achilles is viewed as the golden mean between the rigid Ajax and the slippery Odysseus, and M. H. van der Valk on "Ajax and Diomede in the *Iliad*," *Mnemosyne* v (1952), 269–86. But taking the two poems together Homer certainly merits the title *philodusseus* ["Odysseus-favoring"] which Eustathius (on *Od.* 19, 583) gives him.

said, as he marshalled the Achaean ranks. Any hint of the ludicrous in this comparison is removed by Antenor's subsequent description of Odysseus's imposing presence. But there is something a little unaristocratic, or at least non-Achaean, in this portrait, contrasting with the tall, long-limbed stature of the other heroes.[3] Napoleon would have looked like that beside Wellington; or Cuchulain, that "short, dark man," among the taller champions of the Red Branch Knights. Possibly Homer meant to imply something more than a personal peculiarity here. It may be intended as an indication of some racial difference between Odysseus and the other Achaeans. Perhaps—but it is a pure guess—Homer regarded Odysseus as being partly a survival of the pre-Greek stock in Greece, an "Aegean" or "Mediterranean" type.[4] At any rate, the physical difference serves to mark Odysseus out as exceptional, without giving an impression of ugliness, oddity, or deformity.[5]

One finds the same distinction in a quite different kind of trait—in Odysseus's unusually frank and realistic remarks on the importance of food in human life. All the Homeric heroes were hearty eaters and drinkers. But, whether by accident or convention, none of them except Odysseus had anything notable to say about eating. Perhaps it was regarded as a plebeian subject, unfit for high-born Achaeans; or perhaps they simply were not inter-

---

[3] Athene's other great favourite, Tydeus, was also a low-sized man (*Il.* 5, 801). Other details of Odysseus' appearance in Homer: he had the normal fair or auburn . . . hair of an Achaean hero, but possibly with a dark beard (see Eustathius on *Od.* 6, 230, and 16, 176, and my notes), fine darting, lively eyes (*Od.* 1, 208; 4, 150), expressive eyebrows (*Od.* 9, 468; 12, 194; 21, 431), large fine thighs, broad shoulders and chest, powerful arms (*Od.* 18, 67–9). See additional note below. Roscher *Ausführliches Lexicon der Griechischen und Römischen Mythologie*, v. 3 [Leipzig, 1897–1902]), col. 639, gives details of post-Homeric descriptions. Many of them present a despicable conception of a hero, e.g., suggestions . . . that he was pot-bellied and . . . snub-nosed: but we can probably attribute caricatures like this to general anti-Ulyssean prejudice. Lycophron's description of him as "the dwarf" (*Alexandra,* 124 ff.) is a good example of propagandist distortion of a Homeric description.

[4] As in Patroni's elaborate but insubstantial theories on Odysseus before Homer. Patroni, *Commenti mediterranei all Odiseo di Omero* (Milan, 1950), believes that there is even some surreptitious anti-Achaean propaganda in the Homeric poems, Homer, too, being of Mediterranean race.

[5] Contrast Homer's indication of the positive ugliness of Thersites (*Il.* 2, 216–19) and Dolon (*Il.* 10, 316).

ested in it as a subject for conversation. It was typical of the average Homeric hero that he was prepared on occasion to ignore the need for food, both for himself and for others. The contrast with Odysseus's attitude is well illustrated in a scene between him and Achilles in *Iliad* Nineteen. Achilles, now equipped with new armour and ready for battle, is impatient to launch a general attack against the Trojans to take vengeance for Patroclus's death. Odysseus objects. The Greek soldiers have been kept awake all night in lamenting Patroclus and in preparing his body for burial. The Trojans, on the contrary, have been able to enjoy a quiet supper and a night's rest. Odysseus, not being blinded by personal feeling like Achilles, knows that unless soldiers get a good meal first they will not be able to fight all day: even if they are eager to continue the battle, "yet their limbs are treacherously weighed down as hunger and thirst overtake them, and their knees fail them as they go." There is both compassionate understanding and Napoleonic common sense here: the spirit may be willing, but the flesh is weak; an army marches on its stomach. Odysseus adds some further remarks on the strengthening and cheering effect of food and wine, and ends by demanding that the army should have a full meal before being ordered to attack.

Achilles' reply to Odysseus's reasonable objection is characteristic: "*You* go and busy yourselves with food: *I* shall not touch a morsel until Patroclus is avenged. And, let me tell you, if I were in supreme command, the whole army would have to fight fasting, too, till sunset. Then, with vengeance achieved, we should have a great supper." What is one to call such arrogant confidence as this—with no thought of fatigue or death, no consideration for himself or for others? Is it heroic, or is it schoolboyish? Is it superb singleness of purpose or callow rashness? Odysseus in his reply deftly and gently suggests that youthful heedlessness is partly, at least, to blame. Addressing Achilles with great deference as "Much the mightiest of the Achaeans" he admits his own inferiority to him in martial valour. But he claims definite superiority in thinking things out. Then after an appeal to Achilles to listen patiently for a moment (Odysseus clearly wants to avoid provoking Achilles' wrath again in any way: but he insists on making his point about the need for food), he emphasizes the danger of fatigue in war, and mildly ridicules Achilles' notion that fasting is a good way for warriors to mourn those slain in battle. Bury the dead with pitiless

heart, bewail them for a day, yes—but those who survive must eat
to get energy for punishing the enemy. Odysseus is trying to persuade Achilles to eat with the others. If Achilles fights fasting
against a well-fed Hector, even Achilles may be conquered. Odysseus's arguments fail, as in the Embassy scene, to overcome
Achilles' passionate resolve. But, significantly, Athene intervenes
later, at Zeus's request, and feeds Achilles with nectar and ambrosia
"so that," the poet remarks, "joyless hunger should not reach his
knees." Thus obliquely Homer, Athene, and Zeus agree with Odysseus's advice.

But the typical Homeric hero would probably have admired
Achilles' intransigence more than Odysseus's more practical policy.
One does in fact find an indication elsewhere in the *Iliad* that
Odysseus had already got a reputation for being too much interested in the pleasures of eating. In *Iliad* 4, 343–6, Agamemnon
accuses Odysseus and the Athenian Menestheus of being quick to
hear invitations to a feast, but slow to answer the call to arms.
Odysseus emphatically denies any reluctance to join the fight, but
he passes over the accusation of unusual alacrity in coming to
feasts. Probably he thought it beneath contempt. Yet, as in
Agamemnon's accompanying accusation of evil deceitfulness, it
may well be that Homer intends us to catch a glimpse here of a
general tendency to regard Odysseus as rather more partial to good
fare than a hero should have been.

This is uncertain. But there is no uncertainty about the attitude
of post-Homeric writers. Attic comedians, fourth-century philosophers, Alexandrian critics, late classical chroniclers, agree in ac-
cusing Odysseus of greed and gluttony.[6] They based their slanders
chiefly on some of his actions and remarks in the *Odyssey* which,
considered out of their contexts, certainly do give a bad impression. Thus in *Od.* 6, 250, Odysseus eats "greedily." In *Od.* 7, 215–
18 he asks Alcinous to let him go on with his supper without
interruption, remarking that there is no more shameful compulsion

---

[6] Among late writers Athenaeus accuses him bluntly of gluttony and greed
(*Deipnosophists* 412 b–d and 513 a–d), alleging that even Sardanapalus would
not have made Odysseus's remark in *Od.* 7, 219 ff., "But my belly ever bids
me eat and drink and makes me forget what I have suffered and bids me fill it
up." Athenaeus ignores the fact that Odysseus is speaking of the effect of
extreme hunger, not of any Sardanapalan cravings. Lucian (*Tragodopodagra* v,
261–2), alleges that Odysseus died of gout as the result of over indulgence. Cf.
Eustathius on *Od.* 18, 55, and the scholia on *Od.* 7, 216.

than that of "the abominable belly" which compels even a mourner to eat and forget his grief for a while. In *Od.* 9, 1 ff., after the Phaeacians have given him a splendid banquet, Odysseus pronounces that he knows of no more beautiful consummation in life than a feast with good food, good wine, good song, and general good cheer. Later, after his arrival in Ithaca, when still in his beggar's disguise, Odysseus returns to the theme of hunger and appetite. He tells Eumaeus that it is for the sake of "the accursed belly" that vagabonds are compelled to suffer all the hardships of wandering from place to place (*Od.* 15, 344–5). Later he tells Eumaeus again (*Od.* 17, 286–9) that in his opinion it is impossible to conceal the "accursed belly" when it is in its full fury: it brings many evils to men, and for its sake men sail the barren seas to attack their enemies. Soon afterwards (vv. 473–4) he attributes a violent assault by Antinous to the promptings of his "baneful accursed belly." In the following book he pretends that he wants to attack the rival beggar, Irus, at the behest of "the evil-working belly" (18, 53–4), but repudiates a suggestion by a Suitor (18, 362–4) that he was good for nothing but gross eating (18, 376–81).

If one remembers that no other hero in the *Iliad*, nor any Homeric heroine in either poem, even uses the word for "belly" and still less discusses its effects, it is clear that Odysseus is an untypical hero in this respect. And it is obvious how easy it was for comic writers to portray him as a glutton, courtly critics as a crudely indelicate eater, and philosophers as a confirmed voluptuary, by concentrating on a few passages out of their contexts. Thus Plato was shocked at Odysseus's praise of banquets, as being one of the finest "consummations" in life.[7] But surely the effusive remarks

---

[7] *Republic* 290B. Probably what most provoked philosophers in Odysseus's praise of banquets was his use of the word *telos* which later came to mean something like the *summum bonum*. Even Heracleitus Ponticus, that staunch champion of Homer against Platonic carpings, felt that Odysseus's remark could only be justified on the grounds that he was not himself but only "the remnant . . . of Poseidon's wrath" when he said it (*Homeric Allegories,* 79). With Plato's view cf. Lucian, *De parasit.* 10, where he takes Odysseus's remarks as praise of the parasite's life. According to Athenaeus 513a, Odysseus's remarks were explained by Megacleides, the fourth-century Homeric critic, as a venial piece of opportunistic flattery based on Alcinous's earlier remark on the Phaeacians' love of music and feasting (*Od.* 8, 248)—which is the most sensible explanation, cf. 8, 382–4, where Odysseus praises the Phaeacians' skill in dancing.

of an after-dinner speaker at a royal banquet are not to be judged
as a solemn philosophical pronouncement. Besides, should not
Odysseus's more sober aphorisms on the harmful effects of appetite in human life be weighed against this? And should it not have
been remembered to Odysseus's credit how he had rejected the
temptation of the Lotus-fruit and had resolutely held out against
eating the Cattle of the Sun? When he eats "greedily" after his
reception in Alcinous's palace, should we not bear in mind that
(apart from a snack from the remains of Nausicaa's picnic in Book
Six) he had not eaten for three days and had suffered terrible
physical and mental agonies in Poseidon's long storm?[8] Indeed, he
had shown supreme self-control during his first supplication to
Nausicaa: he had never mentioned food, but modestly asked only
for a scrap of clothing and for information about the city. One almost loses patience with armchair critics who censure the conduct
of a ravenous shipwrecked mariner for not conforming with the
court etiquette of Alexandria or Versailles, and with moralists who
demand the scruples of the confessional in the speeches of the ban-
queting-hall.

Odysseus's remarks on food in the second half of the *Odyssey*
were less criticized, because he was obviously playing up to his rôle
as a beggar in all of them. Further, as the Cynics noticed, he was a
philosophical beggar. He showed that he understood the effects of
appetitite on men in general: how it drives men to war as well as
to trade; how it moves the languid fingers of the courtier as well as
the clutching fists of the starveling outcast. Yet he never suggested,
as the more cynical Cynics did, that the belly was lord of all, and
that he and his dog Argos were equally its slaves. He simply accepted it as one of the inescapable elemental forces in human life.
Heroes like Agamemnon, Ajax, and Achilles, who had, as far as we
know, never been compulsorily deprived of food in their lives,
could nonchalantly disregard its demands. But Odysseus, by the
time of his return to Ithaca, had become painfully familiar with
the effects of involuntary hunger. Homer himself, if he was a bard

[8] There is a choice modern example of this out-of-context criticism in a
recent (1948) study of the Homeric poems: Odysseus's voracity in *Od.* 6 and
7 is explained as a "propitiatory rite." Is it unreasonable to insist, in the light
of both common experience and Odysseus's own reiterated statements, on a
simpler explanation—that extreme hunger compels men to eat grossly?

wandering from audience to audience "for the sake of the accursed belly," may well have made Odysseus his own spokesman here. He, too, if we can deduce his personal feelings from the vivid description of the blind bard Demodocus in *Od.* 8, 62 ff., appreciated the comfort of having a basket of food and a cup of wine within reach to take "whenever his spirit prompted him."

The contrast here between the conventional hero's insouciance, or reticence, on the subject of food and Odysseus's frequent attention to it is one of the best illustrations of Odysseus's unconventionality as a hero. But Homer, perhaps for fear that his less philosophical hearers might fail to appreciate this kind of example, also exemplified Odysseus's uniqueness in a small matter that all warriors would notice. It is frequently emphasized in the *Odyssey* (and also mentioned in *Iliad* Ten) that Odysseus had unusual skill as an archer. His triumph over the Suitors at the end of the *Odyssey* depended on this. But only a few, and those not the most illustrious, of the other heroes at Troy show any interest in the use of the bow. Indeed, there are some indications that archery was despised as plebeian or unmanly,[9] much as a medieval knight of the sword and lance scorned to assail another knight with arrows. Perhaps Odysseus was merely old fashioned in his military technique. Or perhaps it was because the plot of the *Odyssey* demanded a triumph by means of the bow. But the trait does also serve to distinguish him from the other chief heroes. Another feature is far more peculiar. It is once mentioned in the *Odyssey* that Odysseus possessed, and so he presumably used, poisoned arrows.[10]

[9] This is the view of Monro, *Odyssey* (Oxford, 1901) p. 305, and others. Shewan (pp. 168–9) questions it, citing Teucer, Philoctetes, Meriones, and Apollo, as reputable bowmen and concluding, "That the bow was in common use as an auxiliary weapon is certain . . . and that it was held in contempt is not proved." Wilamowitz suggested that *Telemachus* (Far-fighter) was named from Odysseus's skill in archery. For the use of the bow by Homeric heroes see H. L. Lorimer, *Homer and the monuments* (London, 1950), pp. 299 ff.

[10] Odysseus's poisoned arrows are referred to in *Odyssey* 1, 260–1. Eustathius and a scholiast on *Od.* 1, 259 ff. suggest that they were necessary for the ultimate slaying of the Suitors, to make every wound fatal (as Heracles killed Nessus with an arrow dipped in the blood of the Hydra). Or they may have been intended for hunting. Murray (*The Rise of the Greek Epic,* 4th ed. [Oxford, 1934]), p. 130, claims to find traces of the use of poisoned arrows in war in some phrases of the *Iliad.*

This, however, like his Autolycan ancestry, is never referred to in the *Iliad.*

Though Odysseus's Homeric speeches were the admiration of every age of classical rhetoric, their excellence is not that of an orator among tongue-tied men. Oratory was a recognized part of heroic training. Thus in the Embassy scene Achilles' reply is fully as powerful and eloquent as Odysseus's pleadings. At times, too, Nestor's speeches in council are as wise and as cogent as Odysseus's. The difference is not one of skill. It lies more in the fact that, when the other heroes speak, their minds are obsessed with conventions and prerogatives or weakened by passion and self-concern. Achilles' wrath and Nestor's tendency to garrulous reminiscences tend to make their orations more effective as expressions of prejudices and personal feelings than as instruments of policy. In contrast, Odysseus's speeches are strictly functional,[11] as a rule. When he shows passion or introduces a personal touch it is almost always because it will help to achieve his aim—to quell Thersites and to rebuke the wavering Agamemnon or an insolent prince of Phaeacia. Those who consider passionate self-esteem an essential quality of the genuine heroic type may find this kind of self-possession mean or machiavellian. But, as Sophocles indicates in his *Ajax,* it is the faculty that maintains justice and humanity among passionate men.

Besides this functional difference between Odysseus's speeches and those of other heroes, Homer signalizes his oratory by a peculiar personal trait. In Antenor's speech, as already mentioned, there is a description of Odysseus's curious habitual pose before beginning an important speech. He would stand with his eyes fixed on the ground, his body and gestures stiff "like an ignorant fellow's." His voice, Antenor adds, was of great power. But he seems to have controlled this Gladstonian organ with the deftness of a Disraeli: his words came smoothly, lightly, continuously, flake after flake like falling snow—perhaps in the quiet, level tone characteristic of adepts in the art of plausibility. The general effect, we are told, was overwhelming. Homer corroborates this impression in several scenes in the *Odyssey,* where he describes how Odysseus could hold an audience spellbound "like a skilled bard." Homer could

[11] Cf. Eustathius on *Il.* 2, 157 and 337.

hardly have paid a higher tribute to his oratory.[12] Once again he identifies Odysseus's powers with his own.

In the later tradition Odysseus was often accused of cowardice. The charge was based less on incidents mentioned by Homer than on others first recorded in the post-Homeric tradition, Odysseus's attempt to evade conscription, for example, and in later versions of his conduct with Palamedes and Philoctetes. There is nothing of that kind in the Homeric poems. But one ambiguous incident in *Iliad* Eight[13] left a shadow on his reputation for courage. The circumstances are these. A general route of the Achaeans has begun. Agamemnon, the two Ajaxes, and Idomeneus retreat rapidly. Nestor is left behind in grave danger. Hector rushes forward to cut him down. Diomedes sees the danger and calls to Odysseus for help in rescuing the old king. "But," Homer records, "Odysseus did not hear (or listen to) his call, and sped on to the Achaean ships." The crucial verb is capable of two interpretations. It was left open to Odysseus's defenders in post-Homeric controversies to argue that Odysseus had simply not heard Diomedes's cry in the confusion of the general retreat. But his detractors could take it as a deliberate ignoring of a comrade's cry for help. Homer's own intention is hidden in the ambiguity. However, no matter what he meant here, he soon makes it clear that none of his heroes attached any blame to Odysseus for his conduct. On the contrary, Odysseus's prestige is at its highest in the next three books.

If one considers the whole of Odysseus's career, a general accusation of cowardice is plainly absurd. In *Iliad* 11, 395 ff., he stands valorously alone against the whole Trojan host. His bravery in the Doloneia is incontestable. Similarly it took the highest courage to

---

[12] Odysseus's power of holding an audience is emphasized in *Od.* 17, 518–21; 11, 334; 13, 2. Tributes to Odysseus's oratorical powers by later rhetoricians are very frequent; see Roscher, col. 640. The BT scholia on *Il.* 3, 216, note that Odysseus's oratory was "firm" or "robust . . . ," the ideal kind, resembling that of Demosthenes, while the styles of Menelaus and Nestor are compared to those of Lysias and Isocrates respectively.

[13] Shewan, pp. 165–7, has refuted the allegations of Geddes and others that Odysseus is deliberately vilified here and in *Il.* 11, 414 ff., by the poet of "the Achilleid"; cf. Houben, pp. 3 ff. Note also Odysseus's firm and effective opposition to Agamemnon's proposal to retreat in *Il.* 14, 64 ff. For post-Homeric tributes to his courage see Roscher, col. 639.

vanquish the Cyclops, to resist Scylla, to overthrow the horde of Suitors. Yet Homer does seem to hint occasionally, not at coward-ice, but at a kind of tension between prudence and boldness. Thus in Odysseus's brief spell as supreme champion of the Greeks in *Iliad* Eleven, he pauses for a moment to wonder whether it would not be wiser to retreat with the rest. He immediately reminds him-self of his heroic duty, and, with a touch of fatalism, unusual in him, fights on. There is obviously no cowardice in this. On the contrary, the man who fully foresees danger and then goes on to meet it is more truly courageous than a stubborn Ajax or a furious Achilles. The best illustration of this tension between prudence and heroic valour is found in Odysseus's attempt to avoid con-scription by feigning madness, to be discussed in a later chapter. Unfortunately it is not certain that Homer knew the legend.

A commentator on Euripides' version of the Cyclops incident has seen something of a Hamletesque figure in Odysseus as por-trayed there. This was possible in the atmosphere of the late fifth century. But Homer's Odysseus is obviously no indecisive princel-ing sicklied o'er with the pale cast of thought. His decisive boldness is made clear both at the beginning of the *Iliad* in his handling of the Thersites affair, and at the outset of his Odyssean adventures when he sacks Ismarus like any Elizabethan buccaneer or Spanish conquistador. He is "the great-hearted," "the sacker of cities," as well as the prudent and resourceful Odysseus. Yet in both these bold deeds his prudence is not entirely in abeyance. While he faces Thersites uncompromisingly, he coaxes, amuses, and flatters the other Greeks. Again in the sack of Ismarus he orders a withdrawal as soon as a counter-attack seems likely. His comrades refuse, with disastrous results. Odysseus calls them "great fools" for not obey-ing his prudent command. But when he first gave it, they, for their part, may well have thought his prudence was mere timidity.

The fact is that, even though no real cowardice was involved, Odysseus's gift for anticipating dangers and his readiness to avoid them when it best served his purpose, did separate him from the normal hero of his time. Whether one admires it or not, a certain mulish stubbornness in the manner of Ajax, a reckless *èlan* like that of Diomedes, a readiness to let everything be turned upside down for the sake of some point of honour in the manner of Achilles, was more characteristic of the early heroic temperament than a prudent resourcefulness. When the typical hero found his path to fame and glory blocked, his instinct was to batter his own or someone else's head against the obstacle until something broke. The gentle Hector and the tough Ajax were alike in this intransigence. Odysseus was no less determined to gain his purpose; but he was far less intransigent. He was prepared to undermine an obstacle or to look for another path, to imitate the mole or the fox rather than the rhinoceros.

In the later tradition, admirers of the simpler, prouder kind of hero will despise this quality, calling it cowardly or opportunistic. Homer suggests no such disapproval. On the contrary the *Odyssey* implies that some such resourcefulness is necessary to overcome the trials of human life in general. Almost all Homer's more intransigent heroes die unhappily, Agamemnon murdered by his wife, Ajax killed by his own hand, Achilles slain by a cowardly arrow. Odysseus, like Nestor and Menelaus, returns home at last to live in peace and prosperity.

Odysseus was also the "much-enduring" man. Among the other Homeric heroes only Nestor, whose life had extended over three normal generations, shared this epithet with him. Why? After all, many of the rest showed great endurance in battle. The answer seems to lie in a special implication in Homer's use of epithets in *poly-* meaning "much." As has been suggested elsewhere,[14] it seems to imply variety rather than degree, especially in its active compounds. The other heroes were "much-enduring" in their own special forte, namely, fighting. But Odysseus and Nestor were men who had shown their endurance in an unusual variety of circumstances: Nestor because of his abnormally long life, Odysseus because of his enterprising nature. Here once again a clash between Odysseus's qualities and the typical heroic temperament emerges. Ajax or Achilles would never have been willing to undergo some of Odysseus's experiences—his three adventures in beggar's disguise, for instance, and his ignominious escape from the Cyclops's cave by hanging under a ram's belly (which was a kind of Trojan Horse stratagem in reverse). In the later tradition Odysseus is accused of ignobleness, even cowardice, for his readiness to employ disguise or stealth when necessary to achieve his purpose. Undoubtedly one

---

[14] The A scholia on Odysseus's epithet *polymechanos* [resourceful] in *Il.* 8, 93, give a long list of his various accomplishments, as ploughman, shipwright, carpenter, hunter, steersman, and so on. Homer clearly admires this kind of versatility.

can detect an element of Autolycanism here. But what was often forgottem was that these various examples of combined resource-fulness and endurance were generally used *pro bono publico.*

We shall see all this argued out in the later tradition. Here it need only be emphasized that without this quality Odysseus could never have been so serviceable to the Greek cause. This serviceability varied from such an ordinary task as that of pacifying the indignant Chryses in *Iliad* One to the final triumph of Ulyssean cleverness in the ruse of the Wooden Horse. But it is the common fate of service-able men to be despised by their more self-centered associates.

All these deviations from the heroic norm are exemplified in the *Iliad* as well as in the *Odyssey.* The next quality to be considered has little or no scope in the restricted Iliadic *milieu.* It needs the more expansive background of the *Odyssey.* It is a quality that points away from the older Heroic Age with its code of static conventions and prerogatives, and on to a coming era, the era of Ionian exploration and speculation.[15] This is Odysseus's desire for fresh knowledge. Homer does not emphasize it. But it can be seen plainly at work in two of the most famous of Odysseus's Odyssean exploits. It becomes the master passion of his whole personality in the postclassical tradition, notably in Dante, Tennyson, Arturo Graf, and Kazantzakis.

This eagerness to learn more about God, man, and nature is the most characteristic feature of the whole Greek tradition. To quote a recent commentator[16] on Dante's conception of Ulysses:

> To be a Greek was to seek to know; to know the primordial substance of matter, to know the meaning of number, to know the world as a rational whole. In no spirit of paradox one may say that Euclid is the most typical Greek: he would fain know to the bottom, and know as a rational system, the laws of the measurement of the earth. . . . No doubt the Greek genius means many things. To one school . . . it means an aesthetic ideal. . . . To others, however, it means an austere thing, which delights in logic and mathematics; which continually wondering

[15] Jaeger, p. 98, describes Odysseus as "not so much a knightly warrior as the embodiment of the adventurous spirit, the explorer's energy, and the clever practical wisdom of the Ionian", and cf. p. 20, "the cunning storm-tossed adventurer Odysseus is the creation of the age when Ionian sailors wandered the seas far and wide."

[16] Sir Ernest Barker, *Traditions of civility* (Cambridge, 1948), p. 6. Reprinted by permission of the publisher, Cambridge University Press.

and always inquisitive, is driven by its wonder into philosophy, and into inquiry about the why and wherefore, the whence and whither, of tragedy, of the State, indeed, of all things.

This eagerness to learn is not, of course, entirely a Greek quality. Every child, scholar, and scientist, shares it. But it can hardly be denied that the Greeks were endowed more richly with intellectual curiosity than any other ancient people. More conservative cultures like the Egyptian and the Roman judged the Greek spirit of experiment and inquiry either childlike or dangerous. But, for good and ill, it has been the strongest force in the development of modern European civilization and science.

Odysseus is alone among Homer's heroes in displaying this intellectual curiosity strongly. There is an obvious reason for this. A spirit of inquiry would naturally get more stimulus from the unexplored territories of Odysseus's fabulous wanderings than from the conventional environment of the *Iliad*. But it was hardly accidental that Odysseus should have had these special opportunities for acquiring fresh knowledge. To him that hath shall be given: adventures are to the adventurous. One may well doubt whether an Ajax or a Nestor would have shown as much alert curiosity even in the cave of the Cyclops or near the island of the Sirens if they had been there instead of Odysseus. Odysseus's personality and exploits are indivisible: he has curious adventures because he is Odysseus, and he is Odysseus because he has curious adventures. Set another hero in Circe's palace or in Phaeacia and you may have some story like *Innocents Abroad,* or a *Childe Harold's Pilgrimage,* or an *Aeneid,* but not an *Odyssey.*

Odysseus's desire to know is most clearly illustrated in the episodes with the Cyclops and the Sirens. He himself asserts that his original motive for landing on the Cyclops's island was to see whether its unknown inhabitants were "violent, savage and lawless, or else hospitable men with god-fearing mind"—almost as if, in modern terms, he wanted to do some anthropological research. It is more the motive of a Malinowski approaching the Trobriand Islands,[17] than of a pirate or a conquistador. But his crew did not

---

[17] A friend has asked me to reconsider this view, claiming that Odysseus's motive for visiting the island of the Cyclops was simply a desire to get information on his whereabouts (as in *Od.* 10, 190 ff.). But the phrasing of *Od.* 9, 174–6 still seems to me to imply a special kind of curiosity.

share this zeal for knowledge. When they entered the Cyclops's cave, the Companions felt a presentiment of danger and begged him to withdraw. Odysseus refused, still eager to see what the giant was like. In describing the consequences Odysseus admits his folly here in the strongest words of self-denunciation that he ever uses (*Od.* 9, 228–30). As a result of his imprudence six of his companions were devoured. It becomes clear later, in the Sirens incident, when Odysseus meets a similar temptation to dangerous knowledge, that he had learned a lesson from his rash curiosity, for he takes great care to prevent any danger to his companions from hearing their deadly song.

But Odysseus's motives in the Cyclops episode were not unmixed. He admits that his second reason for wanting to meet the ogre was a hope of extracting some guest-gifts from him—acquisitiveness as well as inquisitiveness. The post-Homeric tradition was inclined to censure Odysseus for unheroic cupidity here and elsewhere. But other Homeric heroes were quite as eager to receive gifts as he.[18] It was a normal part of heroic etiquette; and in general the Greeks always had a flair for trade as well as for science. Odysseus's fault lay not in his hope of getting gifts but in his allowing that hope (combined with curiosity) to endanger the lives of his companions. Homer left it to others to draw a moral.

But there is a deeper difficulty in this incident. To anyone who has followed Odysseus's career from the beginning of the *Iliad* up to his encounter with the Cyclops, Odysseus's general lack of prudence and self-control in it must seem quite uncharacteristic of his usual conduct, especially his foolhardy boastfulness[19] after his

---

[18] Aelian, *Var. Hist.* 4, 20, observes that both Menelaus and Odysseus resembled Phoenician merchants in the way they acquired wealth on their travels: cf. the young Phaeacian's taunt against Odysseus in *Od.* 8, 161–4. Comments on Odysseus's love of gifts will be found in the scholia on *Od.* 7, 225; 13, 103; and in Eustathius on *Od.* 10, 571. Plutarch, in *How to study poetry*, 27, explains why Odysseus need not necessarily be convicted of avariciousness in checking his Phaeacian gifts so carefully on his arrival in Ithaca (*Od.* 13, 215 ff.): he may simply have wished to see if the Phaeacians were honest and truthful men; or for rejoicing at Penelope's receiving of gifts (*Od.* 18, 281–2): he may merely have been glad at the Suitors' over-confidence. But both excuses are rather weak. It is better to admit that Odysseus, like the other heroes of his time, delighted in acquiring wealth.

[19] The scholiast ad loc, admits that this was "over quarrelsome" . . . but adds that it would give some consolation to the injured feelings of the Greeks.

escape from the Cyclops's clutches (*Od.* 9, 490 ff.). By this last imprudence, despite his companions' entreaties, he nearly brought disaster on them all from the Monster's missiles. Perhaps the explanation is that this particular episode retains much of its pre-Homeric shape and ethos. It may have been fairly fully worked out before Homer incorporated it into his poem.[20] Its outline is almost pure folklore. Homer's additions seem to consist mainly of vivid descriptions of scenery and the motivation of Odysseus's conduct. In order to fit Odysseus into the traditional plot, and also in order to make him incur the wrath of Poseidon, Homer may have had to strain his own conception of Odysseus's character more than elsewhere. So while in one way the victory over the Cyclops was Odysseus's greatest Autolycan triumph—especially in the typically Autolycan equivocation of his No-man formula—it was also his greatest failure as the favourite of Athene. And, significantly, by provoking Poseidon's enmity it was the main cause of his losing Athene's personal protection for nine years. In other words, in this episode Odysseus relapses for a while nearer to his original character as the Wily Lad than anywhere else in the Homeric poems.

To return to Odysseus's intellectual curiosity: it is presented in a much purer light in his encounter with the Sirens. Here no greed for gain, or indifference to his companions' safety, intrudes. Circe (who in Athene's absence takes her place for a while in advising Odysseus) has warned Odysseus of the Sirens' fatal attractions, telling him of "the great heap of men rotting on their bones" which lies in the flowery meadow beside them. Better not to hear their seductive song at all; but if he, Odysseus, cannot resist a desire to hear it—and Circe knows Odysseus well enough to expect that he cannot resist it—he must fill his comrades' ears with wax and have himself bound tightly to the mast.

What happens in the actual encounter became one of the most famous stories in European literature and a rich source of allegori-

---

[20] A far-reaching problem opens up here; and a greater emphasis on Homer's debt to his predecessors would demand a quite different view of the characterization of Odysseus in *Od.* 9-12. But I must leave it to others to explore this line of interpretation. See D. L. Page, "Odysseus and Polyphemus," *Latin Teaching,* 1949, 8-26, and, more generally, D. Muelder in *Hermes* xxxviii (1903), for possible signs of imperfectly digested material in the Cyclops incident. C. C. van Essen in *Mnemosyne* lviii (1930), 302-8, suggests an Etruscan origin for the Cyclops and Odysseus.

cal and symbolical interpretations. Its significance for the present study lies in the nature of the Sirens' temptation. This was not based on any amorous enticements. Instead the Sirens offered information about the Trojan war and knowledge of "whatever has happened on the wide, fertile earth." To put it in modern jargon, the Sirens guaranteed to supply a global news-service[21] to their clients, an almost irresistible attraction to the typical Greek whose chief delight, as observed in the Acts of the Apostles (xvii.21) was "to tell or to hear some new thing."

As Homer describes the incident, the attractions of the Sirens were primarily intellectual. Merely sensual pleasures would not, Homer implies (and Cicero[22] later insists), have allured him so strongly. He had resisted the temptation to taste of the fruit of the Lotus. But one must not overlook, with Cicero, the effect of their melodious song and their unrivalled voices. Music for the Greeks was the most moving of the arts. Besides, as Montaigne observes in his essay on *Glory,* there was a subtle touch of flattery in their first words:

> Deca vers nous, deca, O treslouable Ulysse,
> Et le plus grand honneur dont la Grece fleurisse.

And perhaps their subtlest flattery was in recognizing Odysseus's calibre at once and in appealing only to his intellect. If an Agamemnon or a Menelaus had been in his place, they might have changed their tune.

For some reason Odysseus's intellectual curiosity, as displayed in his encounter with the Sirens, was not much emphasized in the earlier classical tradition. Presumably so typical a quality of the early Greeks (as distinct from the Achaean heroes) was taken for granted. But the later allegorists, both pagan and Christian, made it a favourite theme for imaginative moralization, as will be described in a later chapter.

It might rashly be concluded from the preceding analysis that Homer's Odysseus was a man distracted by psychological conflicts

---

[21] For the Sirens as a kind of 'poetical gazette' see Allen, *Homer, the origins and transmission* (Oxford, 1924), p. 142, n. 1, who quotes Sextus Empiricus, *Adv. math.* 1. Cf. Athenaeus, 1, 14d.

[22] Cicero, *De finibus* 5, 18. . . . For the view that the Sirens appealed especially to those ambitious for *aretê* see Xenophon, *Memorabilia* 2, 6, 11.

and distressed by social tensions. The general impression derived from the Homeric poems suggests nothing of the kind. The inner and outer tensions are skilfully implied, but the total portrait is that of a man well integrated both in his own temperament and with his environment. As Athene emphasized, he was essentially "self-possessed," fully able to control conflicting passions and motives. His psychological tensions never reach a breaking-point. They serve rather to give him his dynamic force. As a result his purposefulness is like an arrow shot from a well-strung bow, and his energy has the tirelessness of coiled springs. Resilience, elasticity, concentration, these are the qualities that maintain his temperamental balance. In contrast the Ajax-like hero was superficially firm and strong. His code of conduct and his heroic pride encased his heart like archaic armour. Once this psychological carapace was pierced by some violent shock the inner parts were as soft as any crustacean's. Odysseus's strength and self-possession did not depend on any outer armour. He could be as firm and enduring in the role of a beggar or in the cave of a Cyclops as in full battle-dress at Troy. This was the quality that the Cynic and Stoic philosophers were most to admire later.

Such was his inner harmony and strength. His conduct in matters of major importance shows a similar purposeful integrity. He had a remarkable power of taking the long view, of seeing actions in their widest context, of disciplining himself to the main purpose in hand.[23] Thus while other heroes at Troy are squabbling

[23] Cf. H. Fraenkel, *Dichtung und Philosophie des frühen Griechentums* (New York, 1951), pp. 123–4. Chaignet, p. 193, sums up his impression of Odysseus in the Homeric poems thus: *au fond Ulysse est un idéal de la vie morale en même temps qu'un représentant de toutes les qualités de sa race. C'est le type non pas le plus sympathique, le plus noble, mais le plus complet du héros grec.*

ADDITIONAL NOTE: The evidence for Odysseus's age in the Homeric poems is inconclusive. Antilochus, in *Il.* 23, 790–91, describes him as being "of an earlier generation and of earlier men" and also as *omogeron*. The last term is ambiguous: it could denote a person in the early stages of old age, or an active old man, or one who is prematurely aged. Considering that Odysseus's only son was then barely ten years old and that Laertes was still active ten years later, he can hardly have been far advanced in years. Antilochus was a very young man and to such even the moderately middle-aged often seem old. If Odysseus was in his late thirties and Antilochus was eighteen or nine-

like children over questions of honour and precedence, Odysseus presses on steadily towards victory. And why? Not, Homer implies, for the sake of triumph and plunder, but in order to return to his beloved Ithaca as soon as possible. Here Odysseus's efforts for the Greek cause are integrated with his fundamental love of home; *pro bono publico* is ultimately *pro domo sua*. Similarly his loyalty to the Companions during the fabulous voyages, and his patience with their infuriating alternations of rashness and timidity, were part of the same enlightened egotism: he needed a crew to sail his ship home. His love for Penelope, too, was, as has been suggested already, not based entirely on *eros* or *agape,* but also contained that *philia,* that attachment to one's normal and natural social environment which underlies so much of Greek happiness. And his piety is the piety of one who wishes to keep on good terms with the gods.

Such mixed motives may seem impure or ignoble to those who take their ideals from self-sacrificing patriotism, or from self-effacing saintliness, or from self-forgetting romanticism. But these are post-Homeric concepts. Within the context of the Heroic Age and perhaps of the Homeric Age, too, this identification of one's own best interests with the general welfare of one's kith, kin, and comrades, with one's *philoi* in fact, was a saving grace for both the individual and society. All the Homeric heroes are egotists; but Odysseus's egotism has sent its roots out more widely into his personal environment than that of Agamemnon, Achilles, or Ajax.

One other aspect of Odysseus's Homeric character needs to be kept in mind at the last. In a way it is the most important of all for the development of the tradition. This is the fundamental ambiguity of his essential qualities. We have seen how prudence may

---

teen, he might loosely be described as "belonging to an earlier generation." This would place him in the late twenties when he left Ithaca and in the late forties on his return home, which seems to fit the general implications of the poems best. On the other hand, the flagrant inconsistency in the implied ages of Neoptolemus (see commentators on *Il.* 19, 326 ff.) warns against assuming chronological consistency in matters of this kind. If *omogeron* meant having a prematurely aged look, as some ancient commentators held, it would be in character for a man like Odysseus: and Idomeneus (whose brother Odysseus pretends to be in *Od.* 19, 181) is described as "half-grey" in *Il.* 13, 361. But the description of Odysseus in *Od.* 13, 430–34, seems to preclude any premature ageing in his appearance.

decline towards timidity, tactfulness towards a blameworthy *suppressio veri,* serviceability towards servility, and so on. The ambiguity lies both in the qualities themselves and in the attitudes of others towards them. Throughout the later tradition this ambiguity in Odysseus's nature and in his reputation will vacillate between good and bad, between credit and infamy. Odysseus's personality and reputation at best are poised, as it were, on a narrow edge between Aristotelian faults of excess and deficiency. Poised between rashness and timorousness, he is prudently brave; poised between rudeness and obsequiousness, he is "civilized"; poised between stupidity and overcleverness, he, at his best, is wise.

Homer was large-minded enough to comprehend a unity in apparent diversity, a structural consistency within an external changefulness, in the character of Ulysses. But few later authors were as comprehending. Instead, in the post-Homeric tradition, Odysseus's complex personality becomes broken up into various simple types—the *politique,* the romantic amorist, the sophisticated villain, the sensualist, the philosophic traveller, and others. Not till James Joyce wrote his *Ulysses* was a successful effort made to recreate Homer's polytropic hero in full. Similarly after Homer judgments on Odysseus's ethical status became narrower and sharper. Moralists grew angry in disputing whether he was a "good" man or not—good, that is to say, according to the varying principles of Athens, or Alexandria, or Rome, or Florence, or Versailles, or Madrid, or Weimar. Here is another long Odyssey for Odysseus to endure. But Homer, the unmoved mover in this chaotic cosmos of tradition, does not vex his own or his hero's mind with any such problems in split personality or ambivalent ethics. He is content to portray a man of many turns.

The Odyssey and Change

by Cedric H. Whitman

... It can hardly be entirely fanciful to see in the change [in Greek art] from the Geometric to the proto-Attic approach an analogy to the shift of outlook from the *Iliad* to the *Odyssey*. This is no mere matter of subject. It involves the whole instinct about the inner relationship of part to whole, of decoration to structure, as well as the basic conception of humanity and its context. The triumph of scenic episode over totality of design is perhaps the most striking parallel between the *Odyssey* and proto-Attic art. Yet the parallel extends also to many details of the creative approach. In the *Iliad*, battle scenes contain many summaries of unknown men slain by unknown men, *androktasiae*; these anonymities are, however, always named, and their little entries, as in the *Catalogue*, pass by with formulaic rigidity, like the rows of identical warriors on Geometric ware. Individuals become visible only through the shape of a norm. But in the *Odyssey*, the companions of Odysseus are treated differently. They fall into no formalized pattern of the whole, and only one or two are named at all. For the most part, they disappear until they have to do something, and are treated, in contrast to the brief tragic histories of the *Iliad*, as simple expendabilities. Proto-Attic art is not concerned to represent generalities of men, but particularities of event; and hence, instead of the typical scene, formulaic yet possibly individualized to a faint degree, there is either full individualization or nothing. Two of the companions emerge as people, the young, heedless and ill-fated Elpenor, and the presumptuous, sane, and slightly insubordinate Eurylochus. The rest are vapor. It is often said that the characters in the *Odyssey* are types, and some are. But they are regularly types of something in human experience, and never, with the exception of Odysseus himself, typical simply of humanity, as are the rows of names in the *Iliad.* No such generality runs through the *Odyssey*: its pictures seize the foreground and thrust out the binding continuous friezes.

Moreover, in the matter of characterization the methods of the *Iliad* and *Odyssey* differ. As described elsewhere, the secondary characters of the *Iliad* find their individuality through a series of subtle contrasts, either with the heroic norm, or with another character, usually Achilles. Personal details, especially of a trivial sort, play little or no part. But the *Odyssey* is directly descriptive, as a rule through illustrative action, sometimes even in minor detail. We learn the character of Eumaeus from his defense of the stranger from the dogs, from his manner of putting food before a guest, from his tears at the sight of Telemachus, from his strict obedience to orders, from his sedulous care of the swine, and a hundred other touches. Here is no characterization by reference to a single formulaic social norm. The poet is interested both in Eumaeus and in his total context; he wants to fill him out. He is interested in the behavior of dogs, too. In the *Iliad* they only tear dead bodies, a purely formulaic function. In *Odyssey* 16 they keep interrupting the progress of the plot with actions which the poet includes, presumably, out of a concern with naturalistic representation: they assail Odysseus, fawn on Telemachus, and whimper with fear at the apparition of Athena. These are real dogs, not symbols of death with disgrace, and they resemble in their vividness a fine proto-Attic sherd in the Agora Museum at Athens, showing a donkey's head, painted and incised, with mouth open in a most convincing and hilarious asinine grin. So too of the details of personal appearance, one hears little or nothing in the *Iliad,* but in the *Odyssey* the hero's dark hair and stout limbs are often mentioned, especially in connection with his transformation by Athena. In particular, skin quality has newly impressed itself on the poet's imagination: Odysseus is darkly tanned, Penelope's skin is like cut ivory [16.175; 18.196]. Such minutiae are unknown to the Geometric *Iliad,* though women in general are "white-armed"; but in the proto-Attic period, the vase-painters were beginning to represent flesh tones with different colors, white as a rule, but sometimes black for men, and it is perhaps no wonder that this new pictorial element has crept into the epic consciousness. Finally, in the matter of landscape and milieu, it is hard to find any descriptive passages in the *Iliad* comparable to that of the island of Calypso or the gardens of Alcinous. Here simple delight in the setting has tempted the poet to sing on and on, regardless of symmetry or waiting issues. New fields of content have revealed themselves, and the older concept of form has become attenuated amid the new preoccupation with the immediacy of life.

The change in epic, however, must not be looked upon as either sudden or radical. The traditional nature of oral verse precludes radical changes. It must be assumed that the bardic repertoire comprised in advance the formulae and other typological materials necessary to produce the *Odyssey* as well as the *Iliad.* The language of the *Odyssey* offers no foothold to the assertion that it is younger. But its motivating artistic concern is younger, and so is its idea of form. Hence it arises, once more, that the creativity of the poet in such a traditional medium consists in the deployment of his given material, which includes not only plot, but also the whole gamut of visionary, formalized detail which was the singers' thesaurus. It is a matter of selectivity and degree, operating in the service of a sharply focused artistic purpose. In the broadest sense, the *Iliad* draws upon the formulae of heroic warfare, the *Odyssey* upon those of peace, the norms of social existence, and of the adventures of long-existent popular folk tales. It is truistic to point out that the polarities involved exist side by side in the *Shield* of Achilles. The tradition embraced it all, and the poet needed to invent little or nothing in order to create either poem. But the principle governing his selection and emphasis must in some sense follow the artistic spirit of the age, and in the *Odyssey* one may observe the new suppleness, the naturalism, and even occasionally the carefree blunders of the proto-Attic times.[1]

[1] These "blunders" are not found in the same places by all critics. Those discussed by Page, *The Homeric Odyssey,* seem to be based, like so many of the analytic arguments of the last century, on predetermined captiousness and ignorance of oral theory. The real formal weaknesses of the *Odyssey,* as compared with the *Iliad,* can be summarized under three headings: (a) occasional carelessness in the use of epithets or other formulae: e.g., "blameless Aegisthus,", 1.29, or the feeble variants on VI.492f. to be found in 1.358f. and 21.352f.; (b) repetitiousness: e.g., overbidding of the hospitality motif, feasting, etc., and especially the genre scenes illustrating the violence of the

If one attempts to fix the date of the poem more accurately, there is evident risk of pressing the argument too far. Yet there is some reason to feel that the *Odyssey* corresponds to the early stages of the proto-Attic period, and not to that phase, well on in the seventh century, when the style was already approaching Black Figure. Startling as some proto-Attic painting may be, it does not represent an instantaneous revolution. Some later Geometric vases show far less rigidity than the earlier ones; lines become sketchy, poses more supple, knees bend a little, the figures gain a little flesh on their bones; the contiguous warriors in a row may not be all in the same position. One critic says eloquently: ". . . a strong wind seems to be blowing against the neat fabric and making it bend, totter and reel."[2] The change is rapid but the steps are observable. Moreover, the new animal motifs seem to be only partly the product of Oriental influence; partly they recall Mycenaean tradition. Later, Orientalism triumphed, breeding sphinxes, griffins, and gorgons everywhere, and thrusting out the last traces of Geometric order. But at the end of the eighth century and beginning of the seventh century, the proto-Attic style clearly had its roots in tradition, and had by no means freed itself utterly from the Geometric. The *Odyssey* seems equally transitional. Geometric design, as seen above, has not totally vanished, but it does "totter and reel." The wind is blowing vigorously, but it has not yet blown away the epic form. If one were to choose a single vase as an illustration of the creative temper underlying the *Odyssey,* the best choice might be the famous Attic Analatos vase, dated about 700. Geometric motifs are still present, notably the frieze of traditional waterfowl. But on the neck, the dance of long-haired girls and men, one with a lyre, responds with pristine freshness to the pictorial

---

suitors versus the piety of the faithful; a tendency toward "talkiness," in short (these passages are, as a rule, individually attractive enough, but in proportion to the whole, they are somewhat waywardly spun out); (c) an occasional awkwardness in handling the complexities of the plot: e.g., the directions of Odysseus to Telemachus in 16.281ff., bracketed by Zenodotus and Aristarchus, but undoubtedly the kind of slight inconsistency which is native to oral poetry. Examples of this last point can also be found in the *Iliad*; the first two appear to be traits of the *Odyssey,* and, together with the general relinquishment of Geometric structure, point toward a slightly altered poetic consciousness, a disinterest in older methods in favor of new . . .

[2] Beazley, in Beazley and Ashmole, *Greek Sculpture and Painting* (Cambridge, 1932), p. 10. Cf. Beazley, *Development of Attic Black Figure,* p. 4.

urge, the pressure of a new awareness in visual experience. It is descriptive, not symbolic. Reserved space allows the picture to breathe, as in the *Odyssey* Homer gives his descriptions as much time as they want. The atmosphere is spring-like and unprejudiced by previous conceptions, and suggests a feeling of direct delight in life which is essentially foreign to Geometric painting. One cannot yet quite see, but one can foresee, the lyricism of the seventh century, the choirs of Alcman and Stesichorus, or the bright vignettes of Archilochus. The *Odyssey* and the Analatos vase both seem to stand exquisitely poised between two ages, not quite belonging to either, but drawing breath from both.

To arrive by such means at a date of about 700 B.C. for the *Odyssey* may seem both rash and impressionistic. Yet the phenomena involved are specific enough: the decay of Geometric design, the arrival at self-existent pictures for their own sake, greater variety and suppleness of individuation, a freer naturalism, and what might be called the opening of surfaces, whether by space in painting or by a more luxuriant expenditure of time in verse—all these are traceable facts and tendencies. What is more, they are tokens of attitude and motivation, the semiconscious theorizing of the artist as he sets to work, and as such they are hallmarks of a time, never quite to be imitated at any other time. When all the necessary allowances therefore have been made for the difficulty both of dating exactly the early pottery of Greece, and of comparing poetry and painting, the period around the turn of the eighth century still seems more reasonable for the *Odyssey* than any date which, by reason of tenuous and superficially more factual-seeming points of subject matter, would push the poem down to a time when it could only have been archaistic. The inner side of artistic creation is what must be decisive, for it alone is characteristic of its time.

One final comparison with the situation in vase-painting leads to broader considerations. The masterpieces of the Geometric Age were funerary, and their memorial purpose is revealed in the death-like quietude of their formality. They have the heroic death-consciousness which pervades the *Iliad.* The focus of the *Odyssey,* on the other hand, is life in all its variety and directness, and again recalls the more lyrical responses of proto-Attic art, where life as daily lived and observed, unmediated by anything but the senses, finds its first expression since the fall of the Bronze Age, and there-

by lays the foundation of the so-called "Greek renaissance." Such
a shift reflects a shift in the psychology of a people. Ordinarily it
is said that the Greek renaissance was a period of rising individual-
ism and the discovery of the self as such. Yet the *Iliad* is a poem of
self-knowledge in every sense as much as the *Odyssey,* but whereas
the latter exhibits a hero whose will is proverbial for its unity and
tenacity, the *Iliad*'s hero is the first in our history to be divided by
the metaphysical paradox of human nature. Achilles allies himself
with equal intensity, both to his own human nature, with all its
concern and commitments, and to that intuition of the absolute in
being and value which is the besetting demon of the spiritual hero.
These opposites can be joined only in the mysterious flame of a
love at once detached and entire, self-discovery in self-destruction.
Achilles stands representative in and of an architectonic world in
which everything is known and in its place, except himself; his
learning of himself is a creating of himself. Death is always immi-
nently upon him, a formative limitation which reveals itself at last
as the inevitable framework of his tragic being. By contrast, the
life-consciousness of the *Odyssey* involves a vastly different view
of the individual soul. In and of himself, the hero is a fixed personality, confronted by no hopeless division in himself; he is equipped,
as if by magic, with every skill which any situation might require,
so that he needs only to deliberate ways and means; in the whole
course of the poem, his celebrated intellect deals with no problem
which can even remotely be called intellectual, and least of all does
he deal with that deepest of all intellectual problems, the self. He
is himself—at least if viewed from one point of view. Yet from
another point of view, the matter is more mysterious. Life's paradox now appears not in the man but in his external experience,
and the adventures of Odysseus, both on the sea and in Ithaca, cast
upon him a constantly shifting cloud of disguise, from which he
never fully emerges until he has revealed himself to the last person
to whom he must—Laertes. And it is by no means tactless of the
poet to have saved Laertes till last, incidentally, for recognition by
one's father is, in a way, the final legitimation which establishes a
man in his world. And it is the world which is the overt concern of
Odysseus. Achilles created himself; Odysseus creates his world, by
risk, choice, tenacity, and action, and the world thus created reveals the selfhood of its creator. By contact with the "limits of the
earth," Odysseus defines, rather than discovers, himself, each

experience involving, and at last dissipating, a particular shade of that anonymity which overhangs a man until his context is complete. Hence in the first part of the poem Odysseus is regularly an unknown man to those who receive him, until by some word or action he makes his identity known. In the second part, his disguise conceals him, except at such times when the truth peeps out a little, for the astute to read. Mephistopheles promised to show Faust "first the small world, then the great," and through such experience Faust expands beyond the limits of his earlier self to a transcendent knowledge. The *Odyssey* exactly reverses this process. Odysseus begins, equipped with knowledge so various as to be in a sense transcendental, in the great world of magic and mysterious, absolute existences, and slowly by determination narrows it all down to the small circle of his own family household. And by contrast with the *Iliad*, where the world was architectonic and the hero the measure of the infinite, the *Odyssey* presents an infinite and rather amorphous world, under the image of the sea, out of whose mists any monstrosity or beguiling vision may arise, while the hero is the measure of fixity and definition. Perhaps for this reason the *Odyssey* has always seemed the more closely allied, of the two epics, to the classical period, for then too the prevailing outlook centered the legislating mind of the individual as the measure amid unpredictable experience, and infinite possibility. Indeed, it was precisely this view of the individual self, not the *Iliad*'s view, which began to take conscious shape in the seventh century, and to create the new lyrical forms. The *Iliad*'s view returns only in Sophoclean tragedy.

It is an unanswerable question how much of this view existed already in the tale which Homer found, and how much is his own emphasis. The nature of myth, or folk tale, is to reflect in external form the psyche's subconscious exploration of itself and its experience. Myths contain from the moment of their inception all the meanings which can be extracted from them. If Homer therefore created a poem in which the hero reveals himself, not so much directly as through the steady battery of experiences which rub against him, the reasons perhaps are, first that the tale he chose included the possibility of such, and second that such an approach would be welcomed and understood by his audience. The oral poet did not compose in solitude and publish at his own expense; he sang for gatherings of friends and strangers. And if one looks for the time when the stream of direct experience becomes of primary concern to the Greek artistic spirit and fills the foreground with the ideated shapes which to the archaic mind are knowledge, it is to be found precisely in this early proto-Attic period, when fragments of Geometric form, a few Orientalized motifs, and above all direct observations of life itself, merged, sometimes chaotically, sometimes into tapestries of vigor and finesse. All these elements merge also in the *Odyssey,* even to limited traces of the Orientalizing tendency,[3] but nothing is more characteristic than the ordering of the self from the point of view of external experience. And this is perhaps why the motif of self-revelation plays so large a part in the poem. To each of these adventures Odysseus must present and define himself, and he has various ways of doing it.

There is a kind of vague progress in the adventures themselves, the earlier ones, beginning with the sagalike attack on the Ciconians, being less fantastic than the later ones. The Ciconian adventure forms a link with the Trojan war; then Cape Malea is the last piece of genuine geography which Odysseus sights until he lands at Ithaca. Shapes of fantasy begin to appear, but in the Lotus-eaters, the Laestrygonians, and even the unlikely Cyclops, one sees only the milder exaggerations of sea adventurers who had, indeed, come upon sleepy shores and wild men of a cannibalistic persuasion. Aeolus also is a god of the Greek pantheon, a patriarchal king. It is only with Circe that one meets the truly magical, and from there on, the Land of the Dead, the Sirens, the Planctae with Scylla and Charybdis, and the island Thrinacia are the stuff of purest wonder in essence, though sometimes touched with the light of Greek rationalism. Odysseus plunges further and further into this realm, always with diminishing resources and friends, until he arrives at Calypso's isle, the utter submersion of identity, save for bare consciousness and the sea-locked will. This is the nadir, the quiet center of the magic world, "in an island girt by the waves, where the navel of the sea lies" [1.50]. Delphi, the "navel of the world," is the seat of all true knowledge, and in making

---

[3] E.g., the baldric of Heracles, 11.609ff.; perhaps the brooch in 19.226ff.; it is noteworthy, however, that the Sirens seem not yet to have become the bird-women of slightly later times. Had they been, the poet would hardly have missed the chance to describe them, as he does Scylla and Cyclops. They simply "sit in a meadow" and sing (12.45), and do not, as in later vases, fly around the ship.

Ogygia the navel of the sea, Homer has given it an aspect of basic, interior truth.

A desperate struggle with the sea brings him again away from the deep world of faery to the Phaeacians, a people gifted with the especial ability to mediate between relative and absolute, human and divine; they live, as Homer says, at the edges of mankind, and close to the gods. Though they are drawn like an idealized Hellenic colony, their name means, or at least could only connote to Greek ears, "dusky" or "shadowy," and their ships are distinctly spectral. One need not labor the obvious resemblance in all this to hundreds of folk tales about heroes who reach fairyland and return only with difficulty, or having returned too rashly to the world of fact and mortality, go a long and racking journey to recover the sources of unfading quality and power.[4] The question is, what has Homer done? In the first place, he has envisioned all this experience as a paradox, as something to be both embraced and rejected not alternately, but somehow simultaneously; and secondly he has embedded it in a larger scheme of self-revelation and the restoration of right order. He has expanded all the psychological and moral implications of the myth into a parable of truth disguised and revealing itself in time.

Odysseus begins by having his choice. It is he who directs the attack on the Ciconians; in the lands of the Lotus-eaters, the Cyclops, and the Laestrygonians, it is his curiosity, not need, which prompts exploration, for the crew in all cases have already satisfied their needs on the shore; and it is the same in the case of Circe, as the companions already recognize to their dismay. Odysseus is driven to these places, but it is he who chooses to explore them. But after Circe, choice vanishes; he is committed to the world of wonder and must go forward, as the sorceress foretells, nor does the power to choose come back to him until he has been with Calypso for seven years. There is a real difference between the reckless, self-reliant adventurer who comes to Circe, and the fate-driven, desperate wanderer who meets Nausicaa. The change, one may assume, lies more in the journey to the dead than in the arts of Circe herself, and it betokens the fading of an earlier and smaller self before the demands of an even more puzzling and vast

[4] See H. Zimmer, *The King and the Corpse* (Washington, D.C., 1948), pp. 76–88; 131.

world of possibility. After the years with Calypso, all former disguises are stripped away, and he arrives naked before Nausicaa, the genius of rebirth, only to begin a new series of disguises which this time he controls and will abandon in his own time.

To some of the denizens of the great world, Odysseus reveals himself, to others he cannot. The Lotus-eaters could not hear him in any case, the Laestrygonians are a mere nightmare. The friendly exchange with Aeolus does not need full narration. But Cyclops is a real test, and after the disguise of No-man, Odysseus cannot resist the hero's boast, and tells his name [9.502 ff.]. Cyclops and he have measured each other accurately, and the name is now in order. Circe, on the other hand, distillate of woman that she is, knows the hero by his power over her, and becomes, from a witch, a woman of gentle compassion who yields to Odysseus her body and her knowledge, and after restoring his companions comforts them with a sympathy unusual in goddesses [10.456–465]. When one thinks of Odysseus's tenacity of purpose, it is well to remember that, in this one case, he had to be reminded by his companions that he was on his way home. After such renunciation, the way home must lie through the Land of the Dead. And thereafter, Odysseus does not reveal himself until Phaeacia. The Sirens, who know everything, know him without being told [12.184]. The shades of the dead know him. In a moment of recrudescent boastfulness, he tries to face Scylla with shield and spear, and assert the self who fought at Troy, but he cannot even see her [12.226–233]. Troy and that whole world is past; he has just come from its ghost in Hades, where the panorama of the heroic life was reviewed in a dreamlike confusion. All that Odysseus has experienced when he comes to Calypso has defined him indeed, but defined him in lowest terms. Everyman has almost become No-man.

When he comes to Phaeacia, Odysseus is in no haste to tell his name. It is wrung out of him, but when it comes, it comes with the challenge of a man girt with knowledge and secure in it:

> I am Odysseus, son of Laertes, who live upon all men's
> Lips with my wiles, and my fame reaches to heaven. [9.19-20]

Having maintained his spark of identity in the devastating glare of the absolute, Odysseus is entitled to speak as he does. If he comes to the Phaeacians as a suppliant, he soon makes it clear that he is their master, or at least that he has a right to the service which they give him. Upon arrival in Ithaca, he begins to build, or re-build, his world. In the depths of Hades, he has heard from Tiresias of the ruinous condition of his affairs at home. The beggar's dis-guise which Athena gives him is on the surface a practical device for reconnoitering and strategy, but it is also symbolic of a con-dition of the self. A beggar presents an image of humanity fallen, entitled by custom and religion to pity, but little more. The arro-gant will not even grant pity, but the knowledgeable will grant much more, in deference to the changes of fortune and the com-munity of all human things. Meanwhile, the self per se lies hidden. Odysseus can rebuild his world only out of those prepared by their own knowledgeability to penetrate the disguise, and he begins at the lowest rung with Eumaeus, the swineherd. And now the self-revelations begin again, not indeed with Eumaeus, but with Telemachus [16.154 ff.]. The modes of revelation tell more than the identity of the stranger; they rehearse his roles as father, hero, king, husband, and son. Telemachus, though he could have had no recollection of his father, had often imagined him [1.115]. The glorious shape which appears before him, when the disguise mo-mentarily falls, seems at first to the young man like a god; when he hears that it is Odysseus, he believes, with youth's credulity, instantly without token or proof. He could not deny the substance of his imaginings; *certum est quia incredibile est,* it could not be too glorious. Argus the dog is just the opposite; to him there is not even a disguise, it is simply Odysseus [17.291 ff.]. Then comes a series of partial hints. Kicks and missiles bounce off the beggar, frail as he seems [17.233 ff., 462 ff.; Odysseus dodges all subse-quent missiles]. In the fist-fight with Irus, Athena once more fills out Odysseus's limbs, to the terror of his opponent, whom he presently half kills with one blow [18.69 ff., 90 ff.]. Odysseus has now established himself more or less firmly in the household, as the official beggar at the gate, presumably in Irus's place. As a quasi-domestic he is given somewhat better attention, and the courteous Amphinomus, who seems so out of place among the suitors, offers him wine. Odysseus, in a speech designed to conceal as much as it reveals, tries to warn him away from the approaching destruction:

> Nothing more wretched the earth nourishes than mankind,
> Out of all things that breathe and creep upon the ground.

> Never a man declares he will suffer evil hereafter,
> Excellence while yet the gods provide, and uphold his knees.
> Yet when the happy gods accomplish misery,
> This he also bears unwilling, with a spirit enduring.
> Such is the mind of men that live upon the earth
> As the day is which the father of gods and men leads on.
> Once I myself had hope to be flourishing among men;
> Many the wanton deeds I did, yielding to strength and violence,
> Trusting in my father and in my brothers.
> Therefore let not a man be wholly without law,
> But keep the gifts of the gods in silence, whatever they give.
> [18.130-42]

On the moral level, Odysseus could not have been more explicit. He has all but said, "Do not be fooled by appearances or the mere present." He even goes on to condemn the suitors and urge Amphinomus to leave. But on another level, Odysseus has summarized the view of the self which characterizes the *Odyssey*: appearances are deceptive, yes; but the mind of a man is as the day Zeus brings. That is, the spirit is formed and defined by circumstances; Odysseus is now a beggar, but circumstances change, involving not only the dropping of disguise, but the reformation of the self. Amphinomus, troubled though he is, takes his place again among the blind suitors, and suffers in the end. Odysseus might conceivably have trusted Amphinomus with the facts of the case, if he really had wanted to save him. But the test is a moral one, and no one, not even Odysseus, can reveal his true identity to a blind man.

Then come the recognitions by the scar. This is a token which would mean nothing to Telemachus, but everything to Eurycleia, Eumaeus, and Philoetius, since they were present when Odysseus got the scar, and it is to them the emblem of the true king. One glance, and they are all convinced of the return of the young lord who slew the wild boar on his first hunt [19.392 ff.; 21.221 ff.]. The sign serves to connect past and present for those of long memory in the household, and to assure them that this is the same master, the only master. To the suitors, there can only be one appropriate form of revelation—the bow. But the trial of the axes, and the stringing of the old formidable weapon recreate another of Odysseus's roles, that of the hero. The suitors are not like the men of old. The beggar whose limbs looked surprisingly stout now slips the string in the notches, plucks it so it sings like a swallow, nocks an arrow, and sends it through the axes. And thunder greets the falling of the disguise [21.404–423].

So at the end of Book 22, the father, the true master, the touchstone of moral order, and the hero have all revealed themselves. There remain the husband, and the son, or heir. One might well ask why, when Penelope hesitates to recognize her husband, does Odysseus not show her the scar, as he has to others, and as he later does to Laertes. The reason is that a scar may identify a person; but it is a poor sign by which to know a husband. Homer is dealing more subtly. The role of husband must be recreated, not merely the man made known. There can be little doubt in any case that Penelope's intuition has long since told her who the beggar is. It has been most persuasively argued of late that the conversation between them in the firelight, in Book 19, is in actuality a cryptic acknowledgment by Penelope of the stranger's identity.[5] No doubt the knowledge is not supposed to be wholly conscious, even at this point, but the intuition is sufficiently strong to induce her to set the trial of the axes and risk having to choose a husband. Earlier events had been conducive to her feeling, for it could scarcely be more than that. The prophecy of Theoclymenus at the beginning of Book 17, and the sneeze of Telemachus, a good omen which greets Penelope's casual words about the possible return of Odysseus, mingle religious symbols of truth with the queen's growing curiosity about the beggar [17.152 ff., 541 ff.]. When her son sneezes, she laughs—a rare thing for Penelope, but repeated later when suddenly, as she sits in her chamber, she laughs "foolishly," as Homer says, or for no reason, and conceives the unaccountable idea of adorning herself beautifully and maddening the suitors into giving her gifts [18.158 ff.]. As she stands before them, she says that she cannot be beautiful any longer since Odysseus is gone, that if he should return, her beauty and glory would be greater [18.180 ff., 251 ff.]. For whom are these words spoken? It is unthinkable that Penelope should deliberately fascinate a hall full of men whom she despises and wishes in their graves. She has adorned herself for Odysseus, and speaks to him, though the foolish, empty laugh shows that she does not really know it herself as yet. The episode ends in the suitors' giving gifts, and Athena, with a divini-

[5] P. W. Harsh, "Penelope and Odysseus in Odyssey XIX," *AJP* 71 (1950): 1–21. For a more full and accurate assessment of the situation, see Amory, "Dreams and Omens in Homer's Odyssey."

ty's usual foreknowledge of how things came out in the end, treats
this as more or less Penelope's motive; but the queen herself ac-
knowledges no such motive, and states quite a different one [18.
158–168]. The final proof comes when the suitors are trying the
bow and refuse the beggar his turn. There is no reason why he
should have a turn; queens do not marry beggars, and therefore
Penelope says to the suitors, with quiet irony, that even if he
should be successful, she will not marry him, but merely reward
him with raiment and weapons [21.312–342]. But she insists that
he must have his turn, and it is pressing the rule of hospitality too
far to assume that she does so without knowledge of who he is.

Why then, if she knows him, does she not acknowledge him at
once, when the suitors are slain? The reason is that the role of husband has yet to be recreated, and so, therefore, does the role of
wife. The mere slaying of the suitors is no more adequate for this
purpose than is the scar on the knee. Neither is the mere appearance of Odysseus in royal robes adequate, though it had been for
Telemachus. Husband and wife have secret signs, which others do
not know, says Penelope; and, somewhat like a new bride, she cannot speak or look at Odysseus [23.105 ff.]. Then comes the recognition of the marriage bed [23.165 ff.]. The motif can be paralleled
elsewhere, but scarcely the treatment. Outwardly it is a test of the
stranger, for only Odysseus who built it could know that the bed
in Penelope's chamber was immovably fixed to a rooted olive tree.
The stranger need only relate the history of the bed to recreate his
role as husband. But even more pertinently, this scene is a test of
Penelope, self-imposed, in order to recreate her role as wife. For
she too must show him that she will have only the man who knows
the nature of that steadfast bed and, therewith, her own nature.
And to this end she has restrained her emotion and kept back her
knowledge. Odysseus tells in full and leisurely detail the reason
why the bed cannot be moved, and at the end asks:

> So now, I tell you this token. And yet, I know not at all
> Whether, wife, it still stands firm, that bed, or already
> Some one of men put it elsewhere, cutting off the root of the
> olive. [23.202–204]

Penelope has feigned much for a long time, and has lived in sundry
false and inappropriate roles, but the burst of emotion which now
overcomes her wipes them all away, and makes her a wife again.

In the scene with Laertes, the poet finds one more variation on
the recognition theme. Odysseus shows the scar, but passes quickly
on to a token more meaningful: childhood memories of following
his father around the orchard. He names the trees which his father
gave him as a child, thus in a way declaring his patrimony, his
knowledge of the land, and his right to it.[6] He recreates, by con-
tinuity with the past and with the land, his role as the rightful and
legitimate heir. And with this recognition Odysseus has, in a sense,
restored his selfhood completely. Undoubtedly, the whole action
of the *Odyssey* is involved with precisely this, but the scenes of
self-revelation strike especially symbolic notes, in that each limns
an aspect of the self in sharp focus, and somehow summarizes the
hero's relationship to the person who recognizes him. The method
is characterization by definition from without, and the self is conceived in terms of its personal and social limits.

Such externality, such objective observation is basic to the
Odyssey's wide range of realistic detail, from mill slaves, swineherds, and dogs to the structure of ships or palaces, brooches, belts,
the tools of a craft, and the kinds of trees in a garden. The sense of
the uncountable possibilities of existence carries with it an effort
to mark off recurrent shapes of intelligibility, through the observation of functions and forms. And so also, the moral design of the
poem, the somewhat schematized view of poetic justice announced
by Zeus in the exordium, is far more an assertion of the validity of
forms and quasi-ritual observances than a real exploration of the
issues involved. The evil of the suitors is a house of cards, carefully
piled up to be knocked down, with the appearance of justice, at
the appointed time. In the case of Amphinomus and Leiodes, the
poet seems to struggle with the story a little.[7] These two men,
technical rather than actual offenders against Odysseus, are slain,
their essential innocence being of no importance beside their position as suitors. On the other hand, Phemius the minstrel and
Medon the herald, whose offices make them sacrosanct, are spared
[22.330–377]. Clearly the slaughter of the suitors takes place on a
level very far from that which views sin as lying primarily in motive

[6] 24.331ff. Cf. Palmer, *Achaeans and Indo-Europeans,* p. 17, who points
out that Odysseus's relation to the land determines him as the true king, according to the ancient caste system of the Indo-Europeans. In the light of this
statement, the last book of the *Odyssey* can hardly be "late."

[7] See above on Amphinomus; Leiodes 22.310ff.

and attitude. Its basis is a creed, the creed of the primitive clan, and if Homer has managed the character of Antinous so that one feels that his death is justified, the scene as a whole remains a massacre, an undiscriminating application of the univocal law of possession. It is very far from the psychological profundity of the *Iliad*, with its questioning of forms, and its insistence on the inner state of the individual. Here one feels that a primitive story—and the slaughter of the suitors corresponds to the ending of many an old folk tale[8] —has resisted the efforts of the poet to moralize and universalize it. It is meant to be a reëstablishment of right order, but an orgy of blood vengeance peers through the moral scheme, the less sympathetic for being committed, unlike the gory and self-destroying vengeance of Achilles, in the dispassionate conviction of moral rightness.

As outlooks change, some pieces of a tradition become less manageable, while others take on a new luminosity. Insofar as the *Odyssey* is, in outline, a folk tale told and retold in many ways, and here incremented by elements from the saga of Troy, it offered special problems which the simple, unified plot of the *Iliad* did not. The *Iliad* spins out, with infinite elaboration and formal perfection, an episode in itself so slight, that by comparison the *Odyssey* seems heavily encumbered by its masses of material, and leaning a little in the direction of that disunity for which Aristotle condemned the *Cycle*.[9] To dispose with skill and transform into meaningful image and scene so vast and varied a tapestry was to undertake, in a sense, to create a new form; and indeed, the *Odyssey* is not an epic in the same sense as the *Iliad*, but, with its openness to all detail, however homely, and its concern with social types and forms, something verging toward the novel. Perhaps for this reason it is the more popular of the two poems to modern taste. But as a work of ancient art, it lacks the perfection of its predecessor. The problems of disposal and transformation are not everywhere solved as one might wish, and whereas one thinks in the *Iliad* of a single miracle, in the *Odyssey* there are many wonders.

---

[8] See "The King of the Golden Mountain," J. L. C. and W. C. Grimm, *Grimm's Fairy Tales* (New York, 1917); "The Three Princesses of Whiteland" and "Soria Moria Castle," *The Red Fairy Book*, ed. A. Lang (New York, 1905).

[9] Aristotle, *Poetics*, 1451a, 15–22; 1459b, 1.

To return to the suitors, for instance, one may well ask if Homer's presentation does not fall somewhat between two stools. A few of them are vivid enough, yet originally they could not have been vivid at all. In the folk tale, such suitors are an immovable fixture, introduced merely to be the wrong men in contrast to the right man. Homer's interest in them, however, puts them on a different level, and his effort to make them real has led him to im-agine them as young oligarchs. Doubtless he found adequate models of highhandedness and violence in the sons of the rich families of his own time, and the contrast between these essentially unheroic dynasts and the mythic individuals in the epic tradition would lend itself to the contrast between Odysseus and the suitors. But the matter occasionally seems to be pressed further, to affect the whole position and purpose of the suitors. They do not, for instance, seem acutely eager for anyone to marry Penelope. As the latter indicates, their method of wooing is most improper, the re-verse, in fact, of the usual procedure.[10] And whereas the assump-tion would naturally be that he who marries Penelope will be king of Ithaca, the idea of a restored kingship seems to be very far from their intentions, either for Telemachus, or for that matter, for one of their own number; the whole idea of "kingship" has become rather attenuated, so that Telemachus can speak of many kings in Ithaca, any one of whom might be king [1.383–398, cf. 18.64]. Clearly the title "king" is losing its meaning, and is taking on the one familiar in Hesiod, namely, "lord of an estate," or "noble-man."[11] Indeed, at one point Antinous proposes bringing the mat-ter to a close: the choice, he says, is either to murder Telemachus and divide his possessions, giving the palace only as the share of the one who marries Penelope, or else to give up their present po-sition, let Telemachus have his whole inheritance as king, and themselves woo the queen properly [16.364–392; cf. 20.215 ff.; 3.331 ff.]. This is to say, that their current actions are leading not to the choice of a real king, but to a division, by force if necessary, of the regal inheritance among the dynastic families. The speech is delivered in a closed council, to which no one of the other inhabit-

---

[10] 18.275ff.; cf. Antinous's speech, 2.123ff.; also 1.289ff., where it is clear that, even if Penelope marries one of the suitors, Telemachus will have to kill the others, in order to maintain his right.

[11] Cf. Bassett, *The Poetry of Homer,* p. 96. . . .

ants is admitted, a detail which reëmphasizes the earlier remarks of old Aegyptius about the scarcity of councils since Odysseus went away [16.361; cf. 2.25 ff.]. Such close communion is after the oligarchic fashion, and there can be little doubt that the original suitors of the tradition have been conceived by the poet somehow in terms of the oppressive oligarchies which supplanted the Mycenaean monarchies. To conceive them so was brilliant, in that their actions thus achieve a pointed vigor, especially to the poet's contemporaries. Yet, when it comes to their annihilation, they must all, after Antinous and Eurymachus, fall back into the shadows of the old tale, mere wrong men doomed from the first, yet now a little too real to be taken as such. The conflict between the material and the conception is not quite resolved. But perhaps it was in the effort to resolve it that Homer introduced the beginnings of civil strife in the last book, and rehearsed the problem in the second *Nekyia.* No one even thinks twice about the slain suitors in the folk tale. But Penelope's suitors have been rationalized into an all too familiar social scheme, and one must finish rationally: the dynastic families make reprisals under arms, and Homer is forced to bring the matter to a close by the direct interference of Athena and Zeus.

Such inconcinnity, little as one may feel it in actually reading the *Odyssey,* seems, like so much else in the poem's artistic conceiving, the token of slightly altered tastes, of new concerns entering and beginning to disintegrate older forms, even as one sees it in proto-Attic art. The form cannot as yet be called disintegrated, but one feels that, given a little more of this interest in the homely and the contemporary, a little more realism, a little more opening of the door to new impressions, and a new form must replace the epic, at least in its primacy. And indeed, the new forms came very soon, oral poetry yielded place to literature, and epic became a scholar's exercise.

But if the *Odyssey* marks the end of the great oral period of Greek literature, it is an end implied by the material, and a few symptoms of slackened technique do not prevent the poem from presenting a final apotheosis of the whole tradition. It is less intense than the *Iliad* and more external in its view of everything, not from disinterest in the profound, but from the distancing and detachment which comes of retrospect from new vantage points. Already by 700, the Greek world was showing a new face, and quicker changes were in progress than any which had taken place for centuries. Colonization, expansion of trade, contact with foreign parts, and hence wider geographical cognizance, the strong growth of oligarchy, a rising ethnic consciousness, and experimentation in all the arts—all these were forces energetically at work from the beginning of the seventh century, and all are, in one way or another, reflected in the *Odyssey.* The subject of epic was the past, but the approach, insofar as the traditional medium allowed, took on colors from the present. Some of these have been described, but the perspective which they create upon the heroic past, the real matter of the poem, is in itself one of the chief notes of difference between this poem and the *Iliad.* Here one is no longer in the midst of the heroic Achaean world; one follows instead a wanderer from that world, a wanderer who becomes more and more generalized through the first books into an image of Everyman in his experience, and in the last books, reparticularized into a commanding but somewhat altered personality in a world which is also changed. The old Achaean world reappears in Pylos and Sparta, in order to acquaint Telemachus with his heritage. One hears high tales of it from Demodocus, but the people to whom he sings are not of it, except for Odysseus himself. We see its representative string the great bow where the new men fail. But it is a thing of the past. Menelaus, Helen, and Nestor, active once, are now only receptacles of memory, glorious or sorrowful, of the deeds at Troy:

> There lies Ajax, scion of Ares, there lies Achilles,
> There also Patroclus, a councillor like the gods,
> There too my own dear son, both mighty and stainless,
> Antilochus, exceeding in swiftness of foot, and a spearman.
> [3.109-112]

If one seeks the Achaean world in the *Odyssey,* it is to be found far in the west, in the Islands of the Dead. The men of bronze slew each other, as Hesiod says, and Odysseus, nearly the last of them, is undergoing changes. The superb and panoramic dream of the *Nekyia* revisits and summarizes it all for the last time, fixing once more in deathly eternity the great persons of the tradition. Sad, but detached, it is an elegy for heroes who had lived in songs for future men; and now, the songs are changing. In the new world of

Hellas, one sees them differently; they are still the verities of the culture, but the immediacy of life itself is already setting them further apart, while a new kind of man, and a new sense of artistic and intellectual form takes the foreground. The fierce purity of Achilles' spirit, disdainful of phenomena, yields place to a heroic conception more available to a time of widening horizons, the man who wades eagerly through the phenomena of experience, to define himself by the limits of action, perception and understanding. The tale of Menelaus and Proteus in Book 4 presents the paradigm: hold fast to the changing, chaotic shapes, and the truth will come in the end.

In the long run, both *Iliad* and *Odyssey* contributed their share to the perfecting of what we call the classical spirit. Embodying as they do the polarities of that spirit, they remain for us the archetypes of the Classical, the Hellenic, and like all Hellenic things, they stand by a structural tension of passion and form, at once mysterious and profoundly clear.

Characterization

by Jasper Griffin

> Homer has the art of revealing the whole character of a man by
> one word (Scholiast D on 8.85).

The question of characterization in the Homeric poems . . . is
one on which much has been written, and it is all too clear how
subjective most of it is, when we see how flatly scholars contradict
each other.[1] I hope that it will prove possible to establish some
general points about the existence in the poems of characterization, and to see how it is used, rather differently in the two
epics, towards the same goals.

[1] I give only a few examples. F. Codino, *Introduzione a Omero* (1965),
137, thinks that Agamemnon and Achilles are so little individual that they are
actually interchangeable (cf. the justified protest of Lesky, *Gnomon,* 95
(1973), 6; whereas Finsler, i, 327, thought that "no more brilliant characterization had ever been given to a person in literature" than is given to Achilles
in Book 9. Alexander Pope wrote that "every one of his persons has something so singularly his own that no painter could have distinguished them
more by their features, than the poet has by their manners"; J. A. Notopoulos
speaks of "the disappointment of the modern mind in the absence of individual realism in Homer's characters" (*TAPA* 80 (1951), 29). Bethe said the
character of Achilles combined "two fundamentally opposed creations by
two great but fundamentally opposed poets," and that it was "an absolute
psychological impossibility" that one poet should have had both conceptions
in mind (*Homer,* 1, 74 ff.); Schadewaldt found his character consistent, with
two "poles," of anger and gentleness (*Iliasstudien,* 135); Wilamowitz in 1912
snorted that "to speak of a character of the Homeric Achilles or Odysseus at
all is a piece of stupidity, as different poets conceive the same hero differently" (*Kultur der Gegenwart* 1, 8, 12). And so on. A list of modern works
on Homeric characters: A. Heubeck, *Die homerische Frage* (1974), 197.

Some people have inclined to deny the possibility of there being in the Homeric poems any consistent characterization at all. Old-fashioned analysts and modern oralists agree on this point. For the former, separate authorship of the different parts into which they resolved the poems made it hopeless to look for psychological consistency; for the latter, the rigorous constraints of the formulaic system must, it seems, prevent the singer from allowing his characters to speak or think differently from each other. Another question of principle arises: How far is it legitimate to read psychology into what happens in the poems, when this is not made explicit by the poet? The analyst Von der Mühll[2] states as an axiom that "to depict characters, beyond the objective wording of the text, did not lie within the intentions or the powers of Homer," while the neo-analyst Kakridis[3] insists, against those who supply psychological motivations for the actions of the poet's characters, that "in poetry only what is recorded exists: nothing else." From the point of view of oral composition, Kirk warns that "the depiction of the heroic character is limited both by the technique and aims of oral poetry and by the simplicity of heroic virtues and vices," and when, despite these limitations, genuine characterization is still found, he thinks it right to express this in an extraordinarily guarded fashion: "These characters achieve a complexity which has the appearance [*sic*] of being consistently developed as each poem progresses. Even so we must take care not to deduce too much about the methods and the scope of operation of the main poets. . . . " It almost seems as though we become so scrupulous that in the end it seems fair to question not only what is not on the surface of the poems, but even what is.[4]

[2] *Kritisches Hypomnema zur Ilias*, 286.

[3] In *Festschrift W. Schadewaldt* (1970), 60.

[4] G. S. Kirk, *The Songs of Homer*, 265. The temptation exists especially for those who pursue the oral theory, it seems. For instance, M. W. Edwards, *TAPA* 97 (1966), 130, discussing the noble passage at 16.104, with its three-fold repetition of the word *ballein*, "throw": "It might be quoted as a fine example of inadequate technique, or as an outstanding instance of intentional breaking of the rules for special poetic effect. . . . " Cf. also ibid., 153 on 23. 182–3. G. S. Kirk, *Homer and the Oral Tradition*, 84: 'Is Homer to have ascribed to him a minute observation of human, especially feminine, psychology? No definite answer can be given. . . . " Against the former, see *ST* in 16.104–5: "The repetition is to create tension, and the effect is above imitation in painting or sculpture." Against the latter, Coleridge, *Literary Remi-*

In this chapter I hope to make three points, of a fairly general character, which together will prove helpful in considering this tangled question, and which also will show the poet at work conferring depth and significance upon his creation. First, characters in the poems can be different from each other; second, they can be seen to intend things which they do not explicitly reveal as their intention; third, they can be complex, in ways which are rather different in the two poems. . . .

The *Odyssey,* as so often, offers similarity and also difference. Odysseus is entertained and loved by two goddesses, Calypso and Circe, and he has to detach himself from each of them and also to say farewell to Nausicaa. With the glamorous Circe Odysseus happily spends a year in pleasure, "feasting on meat inexhaustible and sweet wine." Eventually his crew urge on him that it is time to go, and he embraces her knees in supplication, begging her to let him depart: his men are melting his heart with their lamentations, when she is not there to see. At once she answers: "Son of Laertes, sprung from Zeus, Odysseus of the many wiles, do not remain longer in my house against your will. . . . " Forthwith she plans their departure.

Very different is the loving Calypso. For seven years Odysseus has been kept prisoner on her island, without means of escape; she wishes to marry him and make him immortal, but he will have none of it. Day after day he sits gazing out to sea and weeping. At last the gods intervene and send Hermes to tell Calypso that she must let him go home. She pours out her feelings to Hermes in bitterness against the gods; then she finds Odysseus and tells him that he can go, if he will, "for I shall send you off with all my heart." The hero is naturally astonished, and she reassures him with a smile, saying "My mind is righteous and my heart within me is not of iron; no, it is kindly." The pair have a last interview, recorded with great delicacy and charm. She asks if he is really so anxious to see his wife, "for whom you yearn every day," and suggests that she, as a goddess, must be far better-looking. The tactful Odysseus at once admits that Penelope is inferior in beauty but says, "Yet even

***

niscences, quoted in J. W. Mackail, *Coleridge's Literary Criticism,* 139, "The Greeks, except perhaps in Homer, seem to have had no way of making their women interesting, but by unsexing them. . . . " There is something which causes dismay about a sort of criticism so nervous of its own subject-matter.

so I wish and long every day to come home. . . . " Calypso never tells him why she lets him go, and Odysseus never knows; she claims the credit for her own soft heart, and in his presence only hints at her bitterness and the real reason when she says "I shall send a favourable wind for you, so that you may reach your home- land in safety—if that is the will of the gods in heaven, who are stronger than I to devise and to carry out."[5] We see through these words her expression of the fact that, were it not for the gods, she would not be letting him go; but for Odysseus that meaning is lost.

Lastly, there is Nausicaa. The night before she meets Odysseus, she dreamt of getting married. When he appears, at first she does not find him impressive; but when he is bathed and glorified by Athena, she says to her maids, "I wish that such a man might be called my husband, living here, and that he might be pleased to stay here!" She goes on to give a broad hint to Odysseus: "If you come into town with me, malicious people will talk, saying 'Who is this tall and handsome stranger with Nausicaa? Where did she find him? He will be her husband next.'" And even her father seems to think the match an attractive one. But of course Odysseus is off home to his wife, and there is no place for Nausicaa. She does, however, manage to be in his way as he goes in to dinner and to have a last word with him. "Farewell, stranger, and when you are in your homeland think sometimes of me and remember that to me first you owe the saving of your life." Odysseus replies that if he returns home safely, "There I shall honour you like a god all my days, for you rescued me, princess."[6] Three scenes of parting, each of them coloured by love, and all very different.

The situation of parting with a woman in love is an emotional and difficult one, which is calculated to bring out the real nature of both parties. It was to have a great future in literature. Virgil's Dido and the *Heroides* of Ovid are among its forms. The variants on the theme in the *Odyssey* show us three very different women: the hard-boiled Circe, to whom the affair has been one of pleasure

---

[5] Parting from Circe, x.460 ff.; Calypso, v; Odysseus never knows her motive, vii.263; "the gods are stronger than I," v. 170.

[6] "I wish that such a man," vi.244. P. Cauer, "Homer als Charakteristiker," *NJbb* (1900), 599 remarks on the subtlety of the transition: "such a man . . . I wish that *he*. . . . " "People will talk": vi.275; Alcinous on the match, vii. 311 ff.; farewell, viii.461.

which there is no point in trying to prolong; the young Nausicaa, with whom nothing is put into words and yet everything is there, in essence rather than in actuality; and the suffering Calypso, retaining her dignity as she loses her love. Each represents a type and offers a different relationship, to which the wandering hero might have abandoned himself, forgetting his wife and home. That he resists them all brings out his unconquerable resolution, the central fact of the *Odyssey*. But we observe also two other things: these women are inscrutable, and they are complex.

Before Odysseus met Circe, Hermes gave him a marvellous herb which would defend him against her magic. When her spell failed to work, Odysseus should attack her with drawn sword, as if intending to kill her; "and she in fear will bid you come to her bed." This duly happens. Circe tries and fails to turn the hero into a pig, recognizes him as Odysseus whose coming had been often foretold, and says, "Come now, sheathe your sword, and then let us go to our bed, so that we may have union in love and sleep together, and trust each other." This is not the behaviour of a fully human person. The immediate transition from hostile magic to the act of love—and after it Circe really is trustworthy—is dreamlike, recalling the transitions in fairy stories. The transformation of a frankly magical tale into one of complex and real humanity is clear when Circe says to the hero, not that the magic herb has protected him, but "your mind is proof against enchantment." Odysseus and his men never understand the formidable Circe. "Now my heart longs to be gone, and that of my comrades, who melt my heart as they wail around me, when you are not present," he says to her, when he begs her to allow him to depart;[7] but she has not the least reluctance in the world. She tells them that they must go to the land of the dead, and the news breaks their hearts. As they make their way to the ship, she "passes them by easily," taking the animals they need to sacrifice to the dead. They do not see her go; as Odysseus puts it, "who could see a god against his will, passing hither or thither?"[8] From first to last she is mysterious, and they are all aware of it.

[7]"Your mind," x.329, cf. Reinhardt, *Tradition und Geist*, 82. "Let me go," x.485–6. The treatment of these lines by G. Beck, *Philologus* 109 (1965), 18 ff., is very forced.

[8]x.569–74. The harsh criticism of D. L. Page, *The Homeric Odyssey*, 32, disregards such points.

When we turn to Calypso, we find that she is inscrutable in a very different way. There is not, as there was with Circe, any doubt or mystery about her basic motive: she regards Odysseus as belonging to her, she saved him from the sea, and she intends to keep him for ever and make him immortal. She conceals her motive for letting him go, as we have seen—a neat contrast with the behaviour of Achilles in the last book of the *Iliad*. Achilles, who told Odysseus that he hated like the gates of Hell the man who thought one thing in his heart and said another, does not try to claim the credit for releasing Hector's body to Priam, saying, "I am minded to give you Hector, and a messenger has come to me from Zeus, my own mother. . . . "[9] She conceals her motive; and Hermes avoids directly threatening her, in case she is minded to disobey the order of Zeus. When she asks, "Why have you come?" he replies, "Zeus sent me here, much against my will. Who would choose to cross so vast an expanse of salt water, without a single city where men offer sacrifices and hecatombs to the gods? But it is impossible for another god to cross or frustrate the will of aegis-bearing Zeus. They say there is a man with you. . . . " On this passage the scholiast comments: "While seeming to defend himself on the ground that it was unavoidable that he obey Zeus, he is really preparing her, too, to accept the facts. For disobedience to Zeus is impossible." He also is too gallant to make any allusion to Calypso's love for Odysseus, saying only that "The wind and wave brought him here, and now Zeus orders you to send him away." It is only the unhappy goddess who talks of her love and her hopes—to Hermes, but not to the hero himself.

Their last conversation is distinguished for what is not said but hinted at.

> Are you so very anxious to sail for home at once? Then farewell; but if you only knew what sufferings are in store for you before you reach your home, you would stay here, and live with me, and be immortal—

[9] "I hate that man, . . . " 9.313; messenger from Zeus, 24.561. There is an exquisite irony in lines v.190–9. Calypso leads Odysseus to suppose that her decision comes from her own kind heart, then she leads him into the cave, and he sits down "on the seat from which Hermes had arisen"—recalling the compulsion she had received in a detail which is significant for us but not for Odysseus. Then they dine. He eats and drinks "what mortal men consume," she is served nectar and ambrosia. The symbolism: they belong to different worlds, to which their imminent parting will restore them.

however you long to see your wife, for whom you yearn every day.—
But in truth I think I am not inferior to her in beauty or stature, since
it is not right that mortal women should rival immortals in form and
beauty.

Such a speech invites and rewards treatment as being psychologically sophisticated. The goddess is saying: "You can go if you want
to, but you would do better to stay with me; I can do so much
for you! I suspect you only want to go because of that wife of
yours, whom you refuse to forget: but I don't see why you prefer
her to me, when I am so much better looking." Such a speech is
not easy to answer. Odysseus's reply could serve as a model for
embarrassed males. He begins by granting and underlining her final
point. "Mighty goddess, be not angry with me; I know full well
that prudent Penelope is inferior to you in beauty and in stature,
for she is mortal, while you are immortal and for ever young." She
is a mighty goddess, he insists, separated by a great gulf from a
mere mortal man; and as for his wife, of course she is far less attractive than Calypso. "Yet still I wish and long every day to go
home and see the day of my return. . . . " The ancients read psychology into this speech, pointing out that Odysseus cleverly began
by clearing himself on the charge of love for his wife, "since nothing wounded Calypso as much as being slighted in comparison with
her," and that he was careful to reassure Calypso that it was not
for his wife's sake that he was anxious to leave, but simply to "go
home." Avoiding any question of invidious comparison between
the two ladies, making no explicit refusal of the appeal she makes
to him in such delicately indirect form, he allows her to keep her
dignity, as Hermes tried to do. The question of principle, whether
such psychological refinements, not explicitly underlined by the
poet, are really to be read into the poem, will be considered after
we have glanced at the scene of parting from Nausicaa.

   We have seen that Nausicaa had marriage in her mind the day
she met Odysseus, that her father was also thinking about it, and
that both of them had thoughts of Odysseus in the role of her
husband. When events take their different course, and he is about
to leave, she contrives to be where he passes and to have a last
exchange with him. "Remember me when you are far away"—"I
will remember you and feel grateful to you for saving my life."
The exchange is inconclusive, on the surface, and yet the audience
feels it to be satisfying and perfect. This is so because we naturally

supply what is not said, what might have been; Nausicaa was ready to fall in love with Odysseus, and hopes at least to live in his memory. She has secured a last word from the glamorous stranger, and she can be confident that it will be something sweet to hear. We have in fact the equivalent, in terms of the softer ethos of the *Odyssey*, of the tragic wish of Andromache after Hector's death, that he had at least "in dying stretched out his arms to me and spoken some memorable word, which I might remember ever after as I weep night and day" (24.743). In the *Iliad*, tragedy; in the *Odyssey*, a touching but gentle pathos.

It is time to confront the question of principle. As we have seen, some people deny that any psychology is to be read into or behind the bare words of the text. This view was heroically supported by Adolf Kirchhoff, at a passage which can serve as a test case. In the sixth book of the *Odyssey*, Nausicaa told Odysseus not to accompany her into town, as their appearance together would cause talk, and even rumours of marriage. Odysseus complies with these instructions and makes his own way to her father's palace. But when her father says to him, "I find fault with my daughter for one thing, that she did not bring you to our house with her maid-servants," he replies "Do not blame your innocent[10] daughter. She did tell me to follow with her servants, but I refused, from fear and respect, lest your heart be angered by the sight; we men on earth are prompt to resentment." What are we to make of this? Most scholars, from antiquity onwards, have seen in the passage a white lie to protect Nausicaa from her father's displeasure. Even Kakridis, in the same article in which he asserts the axiom that "in poetry only what is recorded exists," says of this passage, "The epic poet trusts his audience to detect the intention of the lie: the girl was to be protected from her father's anger," and only Kirchhoff insisted that "If Homer meant to make Odysseus act chivalrously, he should have said so; this is not psychologically subtle, it is merely slapdash."[11]

Now, there are passages in the *Odyssey* in which the poet does explicitly tell us of a character's hidden motive. At the simplest

[10] This seems to be the meaning of *amumona* here, despite A. Amory Parry, *Blameless Aegisthus* (1973), 121 ff.

[11] Kakridis in *Festschrift W. Schadewaldt* (1970), 53; A. Kirchhoff, *Die homerische Odyssee*, 2d ed. We observe that Kirchhoff's method also led him to delete v.103–4, which makes Hermes' speech pointless.

level there is the hypocrisy of a character like Eurymachus, who
swears to Penelope that no man will lay hands on Telemachus
while he is alive, or his blood will spurt round Eurymachus's spear;
he has not forgotten the kindness of Odysseus towards him when
he was a child. "So he spoke to cheer her, but he himself was
planning Telemachus's destruction."[12] Odysseus is famous for his
power to conceal his feelings, and one of the constant pleasures of
the poem is observing him as he does things which have a secret
meaning for him, unknown to the other characters; from asking,
when incognito, for the song of the Wooden Horse, "which Odysseus brought into Troy," to serving as a beggarly hanger-on in his
own home and saying, "I too once was wealthy and had a fine
house."[13] Achilles, who himself always speaks from the heart, is
aware that others do not.

More specifically, the poems contain examples of tact and delicacy, marked as such. Athena comes to Nausicaa in a dream and
tells her that she should take a party of maids and friends on a
day's laundry by the river: "Your wedding day is near at hand,
when you must have clean clothes to wear. . . . the cream of the
young men of Phaeacia are seeking your hand. . . . " The real motive of the goddess is of course to get Nausicaa and her company
to the isolated spot where Odysseus is in urgent need of her help,
but she prefers to go about it indirectly. Nausicaa is delighted with
the idea of the excursion, and asks her father for a waggon for the
day. She does not mention her own marriage, but instead says that
her brothers are constantly going to dances, her father needs to be
well dressed, and she herself has many dirty things. "So she spoke,
for she felt shame about mentioning lusty marriage to her father;
but he understood it all. . . . "[14] Here we have a whole net of unspoken feelings and reticences. Athena acts indirectly, Nausicaa
says something other than what she means, her father sees through
the screen but makes no comment upon it.

---

[12] vi.448, cf. also e.g. xiii.254, xiv.459 = xv.304, xviii.51, xviii.283, and,
in the *Iliad*, 10.240, where Agamemnon tries to protect his brother from
going on a dangerous mission, saying something which conceals his real purpose.

[13] viii.494, xvii.419 = xix.75. A. Roemer, *Homerische Aufsätze* (1914), 90,
discusses this sort of irony.

[14] The opening scene of vi, esp. lines 66-7; cf. H. Erbse, *Beiträge zum
Verständnis der Od.*, 21-3.

Slightly less explicit is the following passage: the first song which the Muse inspires Demodocus to sing among the Phaeacians is the story of a great quarrel at Troy between Odysseus and Achilles. The rest of the audience is delighted with the song, but Odysseus himself, for whom it has an unsuspected and personal meaning, hides his face in his garment and weeps. "Then the other Phaeacians did not observe that he was shedding tears, but Alcinous alone observed it, sitting beside him, and heard his deep sighs. At once he spoke out among the Phaeacian oarsmen, 'Listen, leaders and counsellors of Phaeacia: we have had our fill now of the feast and the music which goes with it. Now let us go out and turn to sport.'"[15] If we press here the principle that only what is made explicit is to be accepted as present, then the poet has not told us that Alcinous acts as he does because he wishes to spare Odysseus, and to do it tactfully. He has not given us, expressly, any motive at all for Alcinous's action. But it is perfectly clear what is meant, and the reader who insisted on more would try our patience. The "white lie" of Odysseus about Nausicaa belongs in the same box, and so does, for instance, a delicate touch in the first book.

Athena has come to Ithaca to rouse Telemachus into action. Odysseus is still alive, she says, on an island in the sea, "and fierce men have him, cruel men who hold him there against his will." Now in fact Odysseus is of course on the island of Calypso, detained by a loving nymph who wants to make him immortal. Who are these "fierce men"? Even in the palmy days of analytic scholarship this contradiction was not seized on as evidence for a separate origin and a different version of the story, because it is so obvious that the goddess is avoiding a truth which, if revealed, would reduce poor Telemachus to despair.[16] These passages help us to understand a more vexed one in the nineteenth book. Disguised as a beggar, the hero has a confidential conversation with Penelope, and tells her that her husband will very soon be home.[17] He gives

---

[15] viii.73–100. On the song, W. Marg in *Navicula Chiloniensis* (1956), 16 ff., K. Deichgräber, "Der letzte Gesang der Ilias," *SB Mainz*, 1972, 18.

[16] i.198.

[17] xix.269 ff. On the meaning of *toud' autou lukabantos*, 305, see H. Erbse, *Beiträge zum Verständnis der Odyssee* (1972), 91. The passage is dealt with excellently by F. Cauer, *Grundfragen der Homerkritik* (1923), 539 ff.: he too is reduced to asking sadly, "Was it necessary to spell that out?" . . . (p. 540, n. 24). He also explains why xxiii.333 ff. do not contradict this view.

her a summary account of his adventures, which he claims to have heard from the king of Thesprotia; and this account entirely omits Calypso, taking Odysseus straight from the shipwreck to the land of the Phaeacians. Analysts failed to resist the temptation here, and "earlier versions" and the like were freely invented. In the light of our discussion we see that the hero spares Penelope's feelings. She would not like to hear from an anonymous beggar that the talk of Thesprotia was her husband's intrigue with a goddess.

This brief survey has shown that the *Odyssey* contains passages in which the poet explicitly tells us of the psychology which we are to see underlying the words and acts of characters, and also that other passages, where this is not made explicit, come so close to them in nature that we can have no reasonable doubt that there, too, the instinctive response of the audience, to interpret the passages in the light of the psychology of human beings, is sound. We need not fear that there is an objection in principle to doing this in the Homeric poems. This does not of course mean that every possible nuance which can be read into the text by perverse ingenuity is really there, nor that we are helpless to choose between plausible and implausible interpretations. The standard must continue to be that of taste and sense, here as elsewhere in the study of literature; we cannot banish them and replace them with a rule, which will give us with objective certainty the answers to aesthetic questions.

Wise Penelope
and the Contest of the Bow

by Frederick M. Combellack

Homer defines Penelope for us in a series of repeatedly emphasized pairs: her main qualities are her beauty and her prudence. Her deepest prevailing emotions are longing for her husband's return and loathing for the thought of a second marriage. Her main activities are weeping and sleeping. Of course, she weaves, like all of Homer's women, but nothing much is made of this. She has no scene corresponding to the picture of Helen coming into her great hall with her maids, her silver work basket, and her blue wool. We are not even told anything about the pattern in her cloth, as we are told in the *Iliad* that Helen's weaving showed the battles of the Greeks and the Trojans. This is the more remarkable in that her weaving of Laertes' shroud is an important element in the background of Homer's story. But even this is kept in the background, and it is not until the very last book of the poem that we are told that this piece of cloth was large and shone like the sun or the moon.

Our problem concerns the character of Penelope, her situation, and one of her actions, as these are portrayed in the *Odyssey*. If the relevant evidence is to be clearly before us, we must examine in some detail some parts of the poem. In Book 19, after Odysseus and Telemachus have removed the arms from the hall, Penelope, looking like Artemis or golden Aphrodite, leaves her room, comes into the hall, and sits by the fire on a chair decorated with ivory

From "Three Odyssean Problems," *California Studies in Classical Antiquity* 6 (1974), 17–46. Copyright © 1974 by the Regents of the University of California. Reprinted by permission of the publisher, the University of California Press, and the author.

and silver, a chair made by the craftsman Icmalius. The scene has been impressively set for the long-postponed first conversation between Penelope and Odysseus, an Odysseus still in the beggarly guise imposed upon him by Athena. The rest of the book is given over to this scene.

The beggar makes a fine impression on Penelope, convincing her that he entertained Odysseus for a fortnight in Crete twenty years earlier. Before, she had regarded him only with pity; now he will be a respected friend. Having won her confidence, the beggar then announces that he just recently heard that Odysseus is close to Ithaca. Indeed, he would have arrived some time ago had he not decided to go to Dodona to ask whether he should return to his native land openly or in secret. The beggar swears an oath that Odysseus will very soon be home. (This is the clear meaning, whatever may be the precise significance of *lukabas.*) "I could well wish that this would happen," says Penelope, "but I think Odysseus will not come home now."

After the longish episode of the footbath (during which Penelope sits distracted by Athena), Penelope speaks again to the beggar, this time in more intimately personal terms. She describes her own miseries during these long lonely years and then turns to the presently pressing problem: should she continue as she has been, staying with her son and watching over the property, or should she marry the best of the suitors? While Telemachus was a child, he kept her from marrying again, but now the pressure from him works the other way; he is concerned about the property which the suitors are destroying.

She then asks the beggar to interpret her dream of the eagle who came and killed her flock of geese and then, as she wept over the dead geese, returned and told her that the geese were really the suitors and that he who was an eagle is now her husband Odysseus. The beggar sensibly replies that Odysseus has himself interpreted her dream for her in the only possible way. "Dreams are hard to interpret," says Penelope, "and those that come through the ivory gate are deceitful. Those that come through the horn gate are reliable, but I don't think my dream came from there."

It is at this point that Penelope announces that tomorrow she will leave Odysseus's home. She will set the contest of the bow and the axes, and the winner of the contest will take her away from the beautiful, wealthy home, "which I think I shall remember even in my dreams." Odysseus urges her to set the contest (and well he might); and Penelope, after a few gracious words to the beggar, goes up to her room and cries herself to sleep.

This scene in Book 19 is enough in itself to make us ask why it is that Penelope, who has waited so long, and who regards a second marriage with such horror, makes up her mind to choose a second husband, when she has just been thinking about this remarkably clear dream (we are not told when she had the dream) and has just received from the apparently reliable beggar the assurance under oath that Odysseus will very soon be home.

There is reasonably clear evidence in the poem that Penelope has long been under considerable pressure to marry again and that this pressure has very recently been greatly increased. Once or twice in the poem we are told that her father and her brothers are eager for her to marry. Some three or four years ago, when Telemachus was about seventeen and might be felt to be at least approaching manhood, there had apparently been a vigorous effort to get her to marry. To avoid marriage, she had hit upon the device of Laertes' shroud, and it would seem that the agreement had been that if the suitors would wait until the weaving was finished then Penelope would, on completing the shroud, choose a second husband. For three years Penelope enjoyed a kind of precarious security, weaving by day, raveling by night, until her trick was discovered because of the treachery of one of the servants. That the trick worked so long says more for the cleverness of Penelope than for the intelligence of the suitors. I think a reader of the *Odyssey* gets the impression that the discovery of the trick and the finishing of the shroud had taken place some time before, weeks and possibly months before. But in Book 24 the ghost of the dead suitor Amphimedon tells the ghost of Agamemnon in the world of the dead, "She finished the web and displayed it, and it shone like the sun or the moon. And at that time an evil spirit brought Odysseus to his swineherd's hut." Amphimedon's words are not only clear, but also emphatic, as the phrase *kai tote dē* shows. We must conclude that Odysseus's arrival in Ithaca followed close upon the completion of the shroud. At the time of the opening of the *Odyssey,* Penelope has very recently finished the weaving, at most only a week or two ago, very possibly only a few days ago. I do not know whether the fact that the weaving has just been completed should make us feel that Penelope should be more willing or less willing to put off the hated decision for another week or so. I should expect that, if anything, a fortnight's delay might seem more reasonable under the very recently increased pressure than if she had already delayed for some time.

It might be argued that what Amphimedon's ghost says is not evidence, because he also tells Agamemnon's ghost that Penelope and Odysseus arranged the bow contest together, and Homer has shown Penelope deciding this by herself. Amphimedon has been drawing a reasonable inference; the reader, who was there, knows that it is wrong. But in the matter of the weaving, the positions of Amphimedon and the reader are reversed: the reader may infer that the weaving was finished some time ago; Amphimedon, who was there, knows it was finished just before Odysseus's arrival. The trick with the web is mentioned by Penelope herself when she talks with the beggar on the evening before the slaughter of the suitors (19.138 ff.), and by Antinous in the assembly in Book 2 (93 ff.). There is nothing in Penelope's words to contradict what Amphimedon says. But critics who reckon up the days note that the assembly of Book 2 took place about a month before Odysseus reached Ithaca. It is unlikely, however, that Homer had kept careful count of the days or even had clearly before his mind just what was said in Book 2. I think, therefore, that it would be unwise to use Antinous's words as evidence that the report of Amphimedon's ghost is wrong.

Another factor which is relevant to our judgment on Penelope's conduct is the prophecy of Theoclymenus. Earlier on this very same day on which Penelope makes her decision, she had been told under oath by the prophet Theoclymenus that Odysseus was actually in Ithaca planning evil for the suitors. Penelope courteously replies, "I could certainly wish that what you say might be true. If so, you would receive such gifts from me that anyone who met you would say that you were a lucky man."

Finally, in her remarks to the suitors in Book 18, Penelope said that when Odysseus left for Troy he told her to marry again if he had not return by the time Telemachus was bearded.

We may now summarize Penelope's situation at the moment when she announces to the beggar her decision to choose a new husband by means of the bow contest:

Very recently, maybe only a few days ago, she has finished the weaving which enabled her to put off the hated decision for some years. Her father and her brothers have made it clear that they think she should marry again, though we cannot be sure when their influence was first brought to bear. She is herself aware that postponing the marriage is unfair to Telemachus, since it involves a steady depletion of his inheritance. And Telemachus is now at an age when Odysseus told her to marry again, though it is not certain either when he first arrived at this age. These are the factors impelling Penelope to take the step she does, and it must be agreed that their cumulative weight is considerable. None of the factors, however, is of a sort to require her to make an *immediate* decision instead of delaying for, say, a week or two if, in addition to her deep-seated reluctance, there are any other factors which counsel a short further postponement. Homer has made the presence of such factors abundantly clear. A few hours ago a prophet has solemnly assured her that Odysseus is actually in Ithaca. This very night, while the beggar has been having his footbath, she has been musing on this dream whose transparent meaning is that the suitors will be killed by her husband. And the beggar, who has impressed her so favorably that he has now become a respected guest and friend, has just solemnly assured her that Odysseus is not far from Ithaca and will very soon be home. An important feature of the statements by the prophet and the beggar is that only a very short time will be necessary to test their truthfulness.

Our problem is distressingly clear: why does the prudent Penelope resolve to marry again at this precise moment when she has no overpowering reasons for an immediate decision and does have these plausible reasons for at least a short delay?

There have, of course, been various attempts to answer this question. One answer has recently been restated by Page and Kirk: Penelope's illogical decision, taken together with some other features of the poem (Amphimedon's story, for instance), "supports the probability that an earlier version, in which the contest was arranged in full collusion between husband and wife, has been extensively but inadequately remodelled by the large-scale composer" (Kirk, *The Songs of Homer* [Cambridge 1962] 247). Whether or not we are prepared to accept this theory, we must, I think, admit that it cannot be disproved. Unlike many guesses about what lies back of Homer, this guess is supported by an unusually large number of details in the poem which are otherwise at the least somewhat odd. The oddities have been well discussed by Page and Kirk, and there is no need to rehearse them here.

Among the Unitarians, the closest approach to this explanation is probably that in Chapter X of W. J. Woodhouse's *The Composition of Homer's Odyssey.* In Woodhouse's view, Homer has reached an impasse in his plot. "Willy nilly, one or other of the actors in the story must do something, in order that the whole thing may go forward. If the poet cannot find in his characters what he needs in the way of motive power, he must just contribute it out of his own head" (pp. 87f). So here, the story must go on, even at the cost of consistency in Penelope's character. For Woodhouse, as for Page and Kirk, Homer's difficulties are rooted in his sources. But for Woodhouse, these are various old "Tales," not a different version of the *Odyssey.*

It was inevitable that solutions such as these should seem to some of Homer's admirers an outrageous aspersion on Homer's craftsmanship. An important element in the derogatory explanation is that in some of Homer's sources, whether earlier "Odysseys" or "Tales," husband and wife are identified to each other before the slaughter of the suitors. We have recently been asked to believe that in our *Odyssey* Penelope really penetrates Odysseus's disguise before she decides on the contest of the bow. This view has been presented in two able articles by P. W. Harsh and the late Anne Amory.[1] I am not sure I have read any suggestion about difficulties in Homer which I should accept with more pleasure than this one, if I thought it were possible. There are, however, two reasons for rejecting it, either of which would be fatal even alone. In the first place, the theory requires us to assume that Homer, regularly the most straightforward and lucid of poets, has chosen to wrap an important feature of his story in a mystery which we can penetrate only by reading between his lines and assuming that he meant things which he did not say. I should think nearly everyone would agree that Homer is not that kind of poet.[2]

---

[1] Harsh, "Penelope and Odysseus in *Odyssey* XIX," *American Journal of Philology,* 71 (1950) 1–21; Amory, *Essays on the Odyssey,* ed. by C. H. Taylor, Jr. (Bloomington 1963) 100–121 and 130–136.

[2] Cf. the remark of Milman Parry (in connection with the possibility of our being able to distinguish particularizing epithets): "if we keep in mind the directness which is from every point of view the mark of Homeric style, and

The second objection to the theory is contained in Homer's picture of Penelope at the beginning of the next book. After her talk with the beggar, Penelope goes up to her room and weeps for Odysseus until Athena puts her to sleep. (Even this does not seem altogether appropriate for a woman who believes that Odysseus is home.) Book 20 opens with a picture of the sleepless Odysseus, who is finally also put to sleep by Athena. But as he falls asleep, Penelope wakes up. She cries and wails and calls upon Artemis to kill her at once, *autika nun.* Better to go down under the earth than to gladden the heart of an inferior man. All this fits perfectly with the Penelope whom Homer has just described, resolved to choose a second husband tomorrow, but hating the thought of it. But Penelope's words are completely incompatible with the Harsh–Amory woman who knows that Odysseus is asleep downstairs.

The most recent discussion of Penelope's conduct that I have seen is that of Agathe Thornton (*People and Themes in Homer's Odyssey* [London and Dunedin 1970] 102 ff.). Mrs. Thornton wisely rejects the idea that Penelope recognized Odysseus before she decides to set the contest. She places major emphasis on Penelope's statement to the suitors in Book 18 that Odysseus when he left for Troy told her to marry again "when you see our son bearded." "Penelope's decision in Book 19 to arrange for the bow contest is clearly motivated by Odysseus's parting words and by Telemachus having grown to manhood." Penelope's decision is proof of "her utter loyalty to Odysseus." So far from finding any bungling in the treatment of this episode, Mrs. Thornton is quite eloquent in praising Homer for the fine ironical way in which he has handled this. The difficulty with this explanation is that it completely fails to deal with the real snag: Penelope's sudden haste at a time when, though she is under pressure, there are no pressures requiring such speed but a respectable number of reasons for at least a brief delay. After all, Telemachus is twenty years old, and his face must have been noticeably hirsute for some years.

We have seen good reason to wonder at Penelope's conduct, but we are not yet through with her. The timing of her resolve to

---

firmly exclude any interpretation which does not instantly and easily come to mind. . . . " *The Making of Homeric Verse. The Collected Papers of Milman Parry* (Oxford 1971) 156.

choose a new husband has been much discussed, and many have found her conduct here out of keeping with her character. But there is another aspect of her conduct which is even more inexplicable.

Homer has portrayed for us a woman whose intelligence is frequently emphasized in the poem, and in Book 23 he shows her more than a match for the brilliant Odysseus himself. He has also emphasized that she is under great pressure to marry again. Finally he has made it clear that the thought of a second marriage fills her with such loathing that even death seems preferable. How is such a woman to solve her problem?

Some years ago she hit upon the device of the shroud. She cannot have imagined that this would be more than a delaying action. Indeed, she must have been remarkably sanguine if she expected the delay to be as long as it actually way. This useful device has now lost its usefulness. What can she do next? The obvious answer, I should think, is look for another device. The really amazing thing about the intelligent Penelope's conduct is that it does not occur to her that she has ready to hand another device which will not merely postpone her second marriage, but will solve her problem permanently.

In the storeroom of her palace, there is a splendid bow, an heirloom from the great archers of an earlier generation. It is an extremely hard bow to string. With it Odysseus in the days before the war used to perform a difficult trick of shooting "through the axes" set up in his great hall. There is every reason to believe that no one but Odysseus (and possibly his son) could string the bow and shoot through the axes.

Penelope's problem almost solves itself. All she need do is pretend to the suitors that she has made up her mind to delay no longer. She has not, however, been able to decide which of her many suitors to choose, and so she will allow a contest with her husband's bow to make the decision for her. It could hardly have seemed unreasonable to the suitors if she added something like, "Since I am willing to choose my second husband in this way, I think it only fair of you to agree that, if it *should* happen that none of you can string the bow and shoot through the axes, you will then abandon your suit and leave my house."

This, I suggest, is the obvious solution that should have occurred to the kind of woman Homer has portrayed. Her failure to think of it has long seemed to me the great defect in the plotting of the *Odyssey*.[3] And Homer could have told the story in this way with only the slightest and easiest changes in the story as it now stands: one or two lines to tell us that Penelope's proposal is a trick and not seriously meant; one or two adding the proviso that will rid the house of the suitors; one or two telling us that after having decided on the pseudo-contest, she woke in the night and was reduced to despair as she wondered if one of the suitors might just possibly succeed. Everything else in the poem can be left exactly as it is. There is no need to tell the beggar that the contest is a trick; the suitors will fail to string the bow; Odysseus will get the bow into his hands, and the suitors will be destroyed. The story told in this form not only saves Penelope from any charge of illogical conduct, but also has a special appropriateness to the extremely intelligent woman we have been assured she is. In the story as we have it, Penelope, the model of cautious, shrewd intelligence, acts on this one occasion like a rash, precipitate fool. It is quite understandable that Homer's readers have often wondered why.

[3] William Whallon ("The Homeric Epithets," *Yale Classical Studies* 17 [1961] 128) argues that Penelope was conscious that the suitors would certainly fail in the contest: "She is called *wise Penelope* . . . when she tells of her plan to choose among the suitors by the contest of the bow and axes, and the epithet and name remind us how she put the suitors off before, and cause us to assume that she plans to do so again. For when we remember the device of the loom, we doubt whether she would initiate a test that she thought could conceivably be fulfilled by the strength and skill of any of the suitors. And if we not only see that the suitors are unable to meet the test, but assume the belief of Penelope that they are all obviously unable. . . . " This assumption seems to me extremely unlikely. It requires us to endow Homer's audience with a kind of clairvoyance enabling the listeners to see what Homer's characters mean at times when they say just the opposite.

In Hades' Halls

by Dorothea Wender

The *Iliad* and the *Odyssey* are works of fiction, not sermons or essays. Like Virgil, like Milton, Homer apparently possessed numerous, varied, mutually contradictory theological traditions to draw on—and drew on any or all of them as needed. The poet of the *Odyssey* (whether or not he was also the poet of the *Iliad*) may have had even more sources to draw from (Egyptian or "Eastern") than did the composer of the presumably earlier work. "No one," says John Scott, "could reconstruct Milton's theology from his poetry, if that poetry were the only source of our knowledge";[1] the same is true of Virgil and, I believe, of Homer. In fact, this state of affairs is less surprising in Homer than in Milton, for the theology of the Greeks was traditionally over-inclusive rather than dogmatic. From a literary point of view there is a distinct advantage in a loose polytheistic system which lacks both a powerful priesthood and a Bible; it enables poets to welcome and use any piece of new or "foreign" lore which seems attractive.

In addition, the life beyond death has always been a fertile field for speculation, since so few of us have been as privileged as Heracles or Dante or Aeneas. As Farnell says (speaking of Patroclus's funeral),[2] "We may indeed say that those offerings are inconsistent with the usual Homeric conception of the disembodied soul as a feeble wraith; but who is always consistent in this dim region of thought?" In 20th century America, believing

From *The Last Scenes of the Odyssey, Mnemosyne,* supplement 52 (Leiden: E. J. Brill, 1978), pp. 26–44. Copyright © 1978 by E. J. Brill, Netherlands. Reprinted by permission of the publisher and the author. Passages in Greek have been omitted.

[1] Scott, *The Unity of Homer* (Berkeley, 1921), p. 134.

[2] [L. R. Farnell, *Greek Hero Cults and Ideas of Immortality* (Oxford, 1921), p. 6–ED.]

Christians can be heard to say "It's as hot as the hinges of Hades," and avowed atheists may refer to death as "marching up to the pearly gates." Each of us probably has his private feelings about the life beyond; some of us, no doubt, have worked our convictions out into self-consistent systems, but publicly we westerners have as common property a large collection of different myths about death; St. Peter guards the gates of heaven in our jokes, but Charon still ferries the dead in our poetry.

Bearing all this in mind, can we deny Homer his Hermes Psychopompus, used only once but used effectively? He does not say that Hermes leads all souls to the underworld, only that he led these souls; the god is introduced here for literary, not theological, reasons. And what are they? I can think of three reasons why the souls should be led by a god, and three reasons why that god should be Hermes.

Why the souls are led by a god: first, the introduction of a deity is the easiest and most effective way to give importance and dignity to any piece of action. Homer is concluding his story; the climax is over, and his audience is perhaps tired, but he has several things still to say for which he wants his hearers' attention. One trip to the underworld has already taken place, and the business he wants to accomplish in this scene is basically human and natural, not mysterious and dramatic as in Book xi. He therefore tries to avoid the anticlimax by a solemn, elaborate introduction. Whether or not he succeeds is an aesthetic question. The general consensus seems to be that he does not (. . . even Van der Valk, who thinks the Nekuia undoubtedly genuine, calls the episode "overcharged.")[3] I disagree, but of course this is not the appropriate place for aesthetic judgments.

Second, and corollary to the first statement, deaths of important characters in the *Iliad* are generally treated differently from and more elaborately than the ordinary deaths of nonentities. As we have seen, most men simply die, meet fate, fly off to the house of Hades, are covered by darkness and so forth, but Sarpedon, Patroclus, and Hector receive special treatment. In Sarpedon's case there is Zeus's indecision and bloody tears and the spiriting away of his body; he is also the first character in the poem to make a deathbed speech. Patroclus is struck by Apollo, then by

[3] [M. H. A. L. H. Van der Valk, *Textual Criticism of the Odyssey* (Leiden, 1949), p. 240.—ED.]

Euphorbus, and finally by Hector; he, too, makes a dying speech, exhibiting prophetic powers: his final release is marked by the pathetic image of the fluttering soul mourning her destiny as she leaves youth and manhood behind her, and he returns to earth as a ghost. Hector's death is marked by the balancing of the golden scales, by the agency of Athene, by another prophetic speech, by the repetition of the image of the mourning soul, and by the miraculous preservation of his body. In similar fashion, the death of the suitors, the only important death in the *Odyssey,* is fittingly marked by unusual circumstances and by divine assistance.

Third, as Samuel Bassett suggests,[4] a guide is dramatically necessary to initiate the action of the Nekuia, to get the souls of the suitors moving. Since their death, in Book xxii, the shades presumably have been resting passively, waiting for Homer to find time to dispose of them; they must now make their appearance on stage, and the introduction of a guide makes their sudden entrance smoother from a dramatic standpoint.

In Book xxii, twenty-one suitors are killed; twenty-one separate deaths are described. Not *one* is characterized by the formula "his soul went down to Hades' house," or by any words which describe what happened to the suitor's shade after death. This might, of course, be coincidence. But it also might be quite deliberate: it certainly *looks* as if the author of the Slaughter of the Suitors (who surely has as much right as anyone to the name Homer) was already planning the Nekuia, and wanted to keep all twenty-one souls in reserve for their journey together in Book xxiv. To my mind, this is important (if "silent") evidence for the genuineness of the Nekuia.

Now, why should Hermes be the god chosen to escort the suitors?

First, he performs a similar function at the end of the *Iliad.* First he is urged by the gods to steal the body of Hector; then he escorts Priam at night on his journey to recover the body. This mission has chthonic overtones, and he is an escort; it is not, of course, *psychopompia,* but it suggests it, and more important is the simple fact that—although generally unimportant in the *Iliad*—he plays an important part in the last book of that epic. If the *Odyssey* is in

---

[4] Samuel Eliot Bassett, "The Second Necyia Again," *AJP* (1923), pp. 43–53.

some ways a deliberate sequel to the *Iliad,* as I believe it is, Hermes' appearance in the Nekuia may be an echo of the conclusion of the earlier epic.

Second, that Hermes had underworld connections in Homer's period is suggested by vii, 136–8, a passage in which the Phaeacians are described as pouring libations to the Giant-slayer before retiring to bed. Farnell[5] (who mistakenly cites the ninth book) says, "The Greeks of the later period had the same custom. Was it not done to secure the god's protection from the terror of ghostly visitations?" Other chthonic connections are suggested by xi, 626, which tells of his escorting Heracles to the underworld, and xxiv, 343 and 445, which refer to him as lord of sleep.[6]

Hermes has a special function in the *Odyssey,* and this is his final bow. It is appropriate that both he and Athene should appear in the concluding episodes of the poem, for the two of them (and not Athene alone) are Odysseus's guardian deities.

Athene's conspicuous absence from the sea-wandering adventures has occasioned some critical comment, for her explanation to the hero (that she did not want to offend Uncle Poseidon) is manifestly lame. Poseidon's grievance stemmed from the Polyphemus episode; why, then did Athene not help Odysseus before (and during) that unfortunate adventure? Surely Poseidon's anger is an excuse of Homer's, put in to hide the poet's real, literary reasons for banishing the goddess. What, then, were the poet's real reasons? Woodhouse[7] suggests that in the pre-Homeric tradition, Athene was absent because it was her wrath which vexed the nostoi of all the heroes; Homer kept the tradition of her non-intervention but changed her motivation. Besides, says Woodhouse, Homer did not want Odysseus to seem like an automaton; therefore, the tradition of Athene's absence from the sea-tales suited his literary needs. Woodhouse presents good evidence for Athene's

---

[5] Farnell, *op. cit.,* p. 10.

[6] Agathe Thornton, in *People & Themes in Homer's Odyssey* (Dunedin, N.Z., 1970), pp. 4–5, has also noticed that the suitors' souls were left, waiting, in the slaughter episode; she also points out that Hermes and Athene are a team in Book i, and that at the end of xxiii, Athene's leading Odysseus and his supporters out of town in daylight is "parallel and contrasted" with the *psychopompia* of Hermes here.

[7] [W. J. Woodhouse, *The Composition of Homer's Odyssey* (Oxford, 1930), Chapter IV.—ED.]

original wrath: iii, 132-6-"Then Zeus devised a woeful homecoming for the Argives. . . . many of them found disaster through the destructive wrath of the grey-eyed daughter of the Great Father," and iii, 143-6, "He (Agamemnon) wanted to detain the host and to sacrifice holy hecatombs to appease Athene's terrible anger—fool, he did not know she would remain unmoved," as well as iv, 502, "Then he (Aias the lesser) would have escaped his fate—in spite of Athene's enmity—if he had not been boastful—," and so we may perhaps agree with one-half of Woodhouse's argument, that in leaving Athene out of Odysseus's wanderings, Homer was following an older tradition in which the goddess actually caused those wanderings.

But why did he choose to follow that tradition as far as he did? After all, he had already departed from it in not making her wrath responsible for Odysseus's misfortunes—this, clearly, because he wanted to retain Athene as his hero's good guardian. Certainly Homer could have departed one step further, actually bringing her into the sea-tales, if he had wanted to. The automaton hypothesis really seems insufficient: Odysseus is no automaton in the Ithacan adventure; although Athene appears frequently, she limits her aid to advice and encouragement, often doing no more than giving divine ratification to her hero's own ideas. A solution to this problem is suggested by Anne Amory Parry.[8] "Athena, as the goddess of wisdom, stands for Odysseus's *total sophia,* and it is appropriate that she does not appear while he is in the process of acquiring the various separate parts of his knowledge." Amory sees the sea-tales as a *Bildungsroman*; Odysseus starts out clever and emerges Wise, and Athene is the divine representative of his wisdom.

There are several good arguments for this view of Athene and of the sea-tales, but a full discussion would not be relevant here. The important point, however, is that additional strong support for Amory's position can be found in the role played by Hermes in the *Odyssey.* For he is the god of the sea-tales, as Athene is the goddess of the Telemachy and the Ithacan adventure. It is Hermes who induces Calypso to let Odysseus go; it is Hermes who gives Odysseus the moly, and who advises him on how to deal with Circe (as with any enchantress); "treat her rough, and don't trust her" is

---

[8] Anne R. Amory Parry, *Omens and Dreams in the Odyssey* (Radcliffe thesis, 1957), p. 86.

his masculine maxim. Although he appears only these two times, they are significant appearances, and on these occasions Odysseus receives more actual help from Hermes than he does from Athene in all her scenes put together. Why should Hermes be the god of the sea-tales? Because the sea-tales present life in a state of wild nature, and Hermes' rough-and-ready, practical "cleverness" is better suited to this uncivilized world than is Athene's "wisdom." Athene's is city-wisdom, the knowledge of debate and counsel and kingly judgment—at its most superficial, her wisdom merges with tact and etiquette, and so she properly accompanies Telemachus on his Grand Tour of the polite Greek world. And why does Athene appear in Phaeacia, although Poseidon's enmity is supposed to follow Odysseus all the way to Ithaca? Because Phaeacia is civilized, because Odysseus has now left the world of nature and violence behind, and now has need of tact, eloquence and urbanity: Athene's wisdom.

Hermes, on the other hand, is feral, and suited to the wild world of giants and sorceresses and cannibals. He is the sly trickster, the god of native wit as well as the god of *techne,* and these are the qualities the hero needs in his sea-adventures. It is, of course, a baser sort of wisdom than Athene's, more suitable for servants than for kings, but Odysseus the many-sided needs and has (at least by the end of the poem) both sorts. He can build a ship if necessary; he can handle women for his own purposes; he can even play the slave. As he says to Eumaeus (xv, 319–21), "By the favor of Hermes the Guide, who bestows grace and fame on the works of all men, there is no mortal who can compete with me at servants' work." Hermes was also the patron of Odysseus's grandfather Autolycus, "the cleverest thief and liar of his day" (Book xix). If Athene is the divine representative of Odysseus's civilized wisdom (or total *sophia,* in Amory's opinion), Hermes represents his natural "wit," his practical talents, his clever dishonesty and trickiness, and just as Athene makes a final civilized settlement with the suitors' kinsmen above ground, it is fitting that Hermes, in making his final bow, should settle the suitors in their last resting place below.

Now, what about the burial question? How can the suitors' shades mingle with the properly buried dead? Page says,[9] "We

---

[9] [Denys Page, *The Homeric Odyssey* (Oxford, 1955), p. 118–ED.]

learn, to our intense annoyance, that the ghosts of the Suitors, whose bodies are not yet buried or burnt, nevertheless enter Hades without delay and mingle with other ghosts. Are we really required to be so short of memory and so slow of wit?"

The dig about shortness of memory refers to the Elpenor episode, which Page takes as theologically contradictory to the Nekuia. However, it is Page who is short of memory; the Elpenor episode actually says *nothing* about the unburied being kept at a distance; Elpenor "comes up" from Erebus with the other souls, and he tells Odysseus to bury him so that the gods will not turn against him, Odysseus. His words imply that it is a terrible disgrace not to be "wept and buried," but that it has any practical consequences is simply not stated. The evidence for this inflexible burial rule of Page's, then, is to be found only in the *Iliad*. There we find, in Book VII, 408–10, Agamemnon saying "I do not grudge the burning of the bodies. For there is no refraining from giving them the peace of a swift fire, once they have died." As in the Elpenor passage, swift cremation or burial is seen here as a kindness and an honor, but the reason why it is so is not stated. The explicit evidence is in fact limited to *one scene only* (XXIII, 72–4), where the ghost of Patroclus says "The shades, images of the dead, hold me apart, nor will they let me mingle with them beyond the river, but I wander thus by Hades' wide gates." Even in this passage there is the possibility that no general rule is referred to; perhaps the shades consider Patroclus's unburied state a particular disgrace; perhaps they let other unburied men in or not as they please.

There is additional evidence that even in the *Iliad* non-burial was generally considered as improper and disgraceful, but not as an actual hindrance to the shade of the deceased. This evidence is to be found in the gods' attitude toward Achilles' mistreatment of Hector's body. Apollo had pity on Hector (XXIV, 20) "although he was only a dead man." Apollo speaks to the gods (XXIV, 35–8)—"and now you won't save him, although he is only a corpse, for his wife to look on and his mother and his child and his father Priam and his people, who swiftly would burn him in the fire and perform the funeral. . . . (54) In his rage, he (Achilles) dishonors insensate earth." If Hector is unburied, then why is there so much emphasis on the pointlessness of Achilles' act? If burial is an absolute prerequisite for the peace of the shade, why does Apollo keep saying "only a corpse," "*merely* a dead man?" Apollo and the other gods do not say that Hector is being cruelly kept outside Hades' gates or beyond the river; apparently their concern with his body is a question of decency, not of theology. Hector's own father does not mention any reason for wanting the body back other than to hold him in his arms and to weep for him (XXIV, 227 and elsewhere).

Thus we find no more Homeric consistency in the reasons for burial than we did about ways to the underworld and no more consistency in the *Iliad* than in the *Odyssey*. As usual, literary motives seem to come first: Homer wanted this scene to take place before the burial of the suitors, because the kinsmen were properly to be dealt with last of all. And what Homer wanted, as usual, he got.

Two aspects of the Nekuia still remain to be treated: first, Amphimedon's incorrect summary and second, the "inferiority" and general superfluousness of the episode.

Amphimedon, according to his critics, makes two bad blunders: he confuses the chronology of the weaving story, and he mistakenly implicates Penelope in the revenge plot. Now just how bad is the ghost's chronological memory? In his speech to Agamemnon, he says that Penelope's trick fooled the suitors for three years, and she was discovered at the beginning of the fourth (xxiv, 142) and forced to complete the shroud. But when she had finished and washed the robe, then an evil daemon brought Odysseus to the swineherd's hut.

How does this account square with the facts given in the rest of the epic? The first reference to the weaving trick is in Book ii, where Antinoos tells the same story in the same words, up to the completion (but not the washing) of the robe. The web was finished, then, at least by the time of this speech at the beginning of the epic. The implication, according to some critics, is that it was completed long before this point: Antinoos is telling an anecdote about Penelope's duplicity in the past. This is an incorrect inference, however, since in the same speech Antinoos says that the suitors have been besieging Penelope for only three years, and it is now the fourth (ii, 89). In other words, the period of their wooing exactly coincides with the period of the weaving trick, and the shroud has just now (in the beginning of the fourth year) been finished. So the length of time between the completion of the web and the arrival of Odysseus is the period between Book ii and Book xiii.

How long a delay is that? It has been frequently recognized that Homer had some difficulty in portraying simultaneous events—for example, the two councils of the gods in the beginning of the *Odyssey* seem to suggest that while Athene is visiting Telemachus, Hermes is at the same time disengaging Odysseus from Calypso. If this is so, then the delay between the completion of the web and the hero's return to Ithaca is not more than twenty-eight days. Odysseus takes five days to build his raft, sails for eighteen, is lost on the sea for three, spends two days with the Phaeacians and one day on the Phaeacian boat, and arrives home in the evening. Less than a month—or, if the two Olympian councils are not regarded as the same council, the time span is slightly more than a month. Surely this is not so long a time that Amphimedon is totally unjustified in saying "when . . . then." In the context of Odysseus's years of absence and Penelope's drawn-out anxiety, a month would seem negligible. Once the question of her remarrying was settled, Penelope would certainly have been given at least a month's grace to make her final decision on *whom* to marry. Just as the weaving plot demands (to be artistically satisfying), the deliverer does arrive in the nick of time.

The heroine herself confirms Amphimedon's view of the chronology. In Book xix, she tells the disguised Odysseus the story of her weaving trick—and after the familiar line "I was forced to complete it, unwillingly," she says *"And now* I can neither escape this marriage nor find any other trick." So it is clear that she, like Amphimedon, considers that the weaving device has just now failed, and that the critical aftermath of its failure is in the immediate present.

Amphimedon does, however, make a real mistake, about Penelope's role in the final event: he says (xxiv, 167–8) "He (Odysseus) in his cunning ordered his wife to set up for the suitors the bow and the grey iron. . . . " As we know from Book xix, Penelope herself devised the trial of the bow. The disguised Odysseus encouraged her not to delay it, but she did not know her husband, and had no knowledge that what she was doing would fit in with his plans; in xxi, she fetched the bow on inspiration from Athene. Amphimedon's story, a more convincingly motivated version than was the actual sequence of events, implies that Penelope had already recognized her husband and was in on the revenge plot. The simplest (and perhaps the best) explanation of this error is

Lang's:[10] "This is merely an erroneous inference of the ghost's." How could Amphimedon think otherwise?[11] Penelope certainly behaved as if she were in on the plot. Although erroneous, Amphimedon's inference is certainly natural enough—otherwise, Penelope's action is incomprehensible and unmotivated. Actually, it was unmotivated—Athene's prompting being, as Woodhouse has seen, a convenient shorthand for "spontaneously, for no reason." As Woodhouse points out,[12] Homer had a difficult problem at this point in the story; if Penelope recognized Odysseus before the suitors are dealt with, her behavior preceding the revenge can be made convincing, but the recognition scene between husband and wife—a high point of the epic—will be robbed of dramatic power. Apparently Homer preferred to save the recognition and reunion for the choicer dramatic moment, after the revenge; he was therefore faced with the dilemma of an ignorant, unmotivated Penelope. He patched it up as well as possible by having her consciously behave as if she knew the truth (as Amory points out),[13] but not without some sacrifice of psychological "realism."

Amphimedon's error, then, is a natural one—his version implies a less dramatically effective plot than Homer's, but a more convincing one. But why did Homer allow one of his characters thus to point up the psychological flaw in his story? Perhaps it is a slip-up on the poet's part—an unconscious reversion (as Woodhouse and Page think)[14] to an earlier or better-known form of the tale. Or perhaps Homer assumed that by this time his audience would have forgotten the precise details of the revenge story and would accept this more realistic plot as a correct summary; in this way, the bard would eat his cake and have it, too: his hearers would remember the striking husband–wife recognition scene, but would fail to notice its incompatibility with the also striking and clever revenge plot as recapitulated by Amphimedon.

[10] [Andrew Lang, *Homer and the Epic* (London, 1893), p. 317.—ED.]

[11] Homer is generally careful not to attribute the omniscience of the bard to his human characters: cf. xii, 389–90 where he painstakingly provides a rational explanation for how Odysseus came to know of a dialogue on Olympus.

[12] Woodhouse, *Composition*, Chapter XV.

[13] Amory, *Omens and Dreams*, p. 173. Also cf. P. W. Harsh, "Penelope and Odysseus in *Odyssey* XIX," *AJP* 71 (1950), pp. 1–21.

[14] Woodhouse, *op. cit.*, p. 70; Page, *Homeric Odyssey*, pp. 121–8.

But this is merely speculation. Whatever Homer's reasons for allowing Amphimedon to blunder, the more important (and often neglected) fact is how much Amphimedon got *right*. It is a long and detailed epitome, so detailed that it is hard to imagine that it could have been written by someone who was not exceedingly familiar with our *Odyssey*. There probably were other versions of the Return of Odysseus current in and before and after Homer's time, but is it likely that any of them contained this precise combination: Odysseus arrives in Ithaca, stays in swineherd's cabin; Telemachus returns to palace first; Eumaeus and Odysseus follow later, Odysseus dressed as a beggar, *and,* Antinoos is the first suitor felled?

No. It is not likely. This speech seems to have been written, whether or not by Homer, for *this version* of the *Odyssey*. Why, then, should any critic worry about the mistake (or mistakes, if the web story is still considered incorrect) that Amphimedon made? The only anti-Homeric argument based on this mistake is that the author of this speech must have been epitomizing a different *Odyssey*; if we grant that Amphimedon's speech was written specifically for *our Odyssey,* then the case against Homeric authorship collapses. (That Homer would be more familiar with his own material than a forger would be is an unprovable assumption—it can be argued with equal persuasiveness that a forger or a rhapsode would be more careful not to make mistakes.)

As has been mentioned before, Amphimedon's epitome is the third of three, and completes the summarizing of the entire plot of the *Odyssey*. Telemachus summarizes his adventures for Penelope; Odysseus summarizes the sea-tales in xxiii and in Amphimedon's speech the poet reviews the last and most fundamental part of the three-fold plot, the Return and Revenge of Odysseus.

The fifth and final objection to the Nekuia is that it is pointless. It interrupts the plot, contributes nothing, and is poorly written.

I cannot, of course, prove that the Nekuia is well written. Those who dislike it will probably continue to dislike it no matter what anyone says on behalf of the episode. I do trust, however, that the large number of lines here repeated from other parts of the epic no longer constitutes a major threat to the episode's acceptance. Shewan has gone into this point at great length.[15] "Knowing the

[15] [A. Shewan, "The 'Continuation' of the *Odyssey*," *Classical Philology* 9 (1914), p. 41.—ED.]

epic way," he concludes, "we expect many pieces of description to recur in the *ipsissima verba* used earlier in the book." In this I concur, and trust that it would be superfluous on my part to add anything more; most critics these days recognize, I think, that formulaic repetitions are not only excusable in Homer, they are to be expected.

What I can and will argue about, however, is the relevance of the Nekuia to the rest of the *Odyssey*. The episode does not interrupt the plot; it complements, contributes to, and helps to complete the story of Odysseus's return in at least four ways.

First of all, as has been pointed out frequently, Penelope here gets her long overdue encomium. She is, after all, the heroine of the *Odyssey*; the most important of the three plots depends on and revolves around her, and her proverbial constancy and "wisdom" are necessary to the happy resolution of the hero's adventures. But until this point in the story she has received no word of praise for her part in the revenge plot, no proper panegyric for her long years of faithfulness, unless we count Anticleia's few words in the underworld. Penelope's praise is particularly satisfying, therefore, when it does come, at this late point and from this particular character. For Agamemnon is not only dead, and therefore presumably more respectable and objective as a judge than Odysseus would have been, but he is also (understandably) a considerable misogynist, who in the eleventh book had called women an untrustworthy lot, and had warned Odysseus to be wary of Penelope on his return. His suspicions now quelled, the hero of Troy ungrudgingly gives Penelope her due: the gods themselves will inspire songs in her honor; her virtue will become as proverbial as Clytaemnestra's faithlessness. How much more pleasing this one late burst of admiration is than, for example, the rather wearying outpourings of the *Alcestis,* which actually diminish that heroine's stature by their excessiveness.

The second useful function the Nekuia serves is to provide a funeral. Perhaps every proper epic of Homer's time included one; we have no evidence on this point. (Although Lord considers laments and funerals to have a special importance in epic poetry generally.)[16] More important, however, is the fact that the *Iliad* does contain an important one, and the *Odyssey,* although its sub-

[16] A. B. Lord, in: Wace and Stubbings, *Companion to Homer* (London, 1962), p. 202.

ject matter and general approach are very different from the *Iliad,*
in several respects echoes that work almost reverently. For example, the games: in the *Iliad,* the funeral games of Patroclus,
although they are dealt with in such loving (and to moderns, excessive) detail, still come at a natural point in the plot. But the
Phaeacian games are really dragged in; presumably they were introduced (like many of the epic's sacrifices, displays of *techne,* and
descriptions of clothing, etc.) either as an epic convention, an already established feature of the poem which the audience would
expect, or simply because the *Iliad* too had its games. Might not
the funeral here described fill a similar function, to entertain an
audience already familiar with and enthusiastic about (or even
reverent towards) the *Iliad?*

As far as funerals go, however, the poet of the *Odyssey* had a
problem: Elpenor was too insignificant a character (compared with
Patroclus) to rate a really impressive rite; the suitors were villains;
and Odysseus himself was not to die in the course of the story.
So—if the epic was to contain a hero's funeral to equal or surpass
that of the *Iliad,* it would have to belong to a character peripheral
to the story—and what better choice than the very hero of the
Iliad, whose final end had been foreseen but not described in that
epic? The story of Achilles is not really complete until this moment; as Sainte-Beuve remarked,[17] "Homère a esquissé en traits
sublimes ce que furent ces funerailles, ce qu'elles durent être; la fin
de l'Odyssée respond ainsi a la pensée même de l'Iliade, et y
concorde par un effet plein de grandeur."

We have seen that the Nekuia provides a last bow for Hermes,
and for Achilles. It is also a farewell appearance of the suitors, and
of Agamemnon, Patroclus, Antilochus, and Ajax. Thus the whole
Trojan story is completed in the *Odyssey*; as Bassett says,[18] "every
prominent Greek whose story was left unfinished in the *Iliad* finds
a place either in the Telemachy or in one of the two Necyias."
And what of the characters of the *Odyssey?* Penelope and Eurycleia
appeared for the last time just before this scene; the rest of the
major characters (Odysseus, Telemachus, Laertes, the two herdsmen, Mentor, and Athene herself) have their curtain calls at the
very end; two living men, however, played important parts in the

---

[17] Sainte-Beuve, *Etude sur Quintus Smyrnaeus,* p. 385, quoted in Lang, *op.
cit.*; p. 317.

[18] Bassett, *The Poetry of Homer* (Berkeley, 1932), p. 175.

plot, and cannot reasonably appear in Ithaca—Nestor and Menelaus. But they, too, have final bows: in Agamemnon's description of Achilles' funeral, Nestor is described as preventing a panic among the troops, who were terrified at the arrival of Thetis and her nymphs. Nestor is singled out for praise, called "the man who knew many ancient things, Nestor, whose counsels had prevailed (often) before this" (51–2). Menelaus, too, is brought into the narrative; Agamemnon reminds Amphimedon of the occasion on which he and Menelaus visited Ithaca. Perfunctory though they are, these references seem to have been worked in deliberately by a poet who was trying to get into the concluding scenes of his epic some mention of every major figure who has taken part in the story. (To be *really* complete, of course, we would have to consider the conclusion of the epic as beginning with the Odysseus—Penelope reconciliation, where Helen is mentioned, or at least with Odysseus's epitome of his wanderings, which lists the chief characters in that part of the story. But this would perhaps be stretching a point.)

At last we come to that function of the episode which seems to be both the most obvious and the most important: the comparison of Odysseus with Agamemnon and Achilles. Character-comparison is a technique which pervades the entire *Odyssey*; nearly every character in the poem can be compared with or contrasted to either Odysseus, or Penelope, or Telemachus. This point will be discussed more fully in Chapter Six; for now, let us limit the examination to Achilles and Agamemnon. Agamemnon's case is the simpler; it has been repeatedly recognized that his tragedy had a special fascination for the poet of the *Odyssey*; it is referred to some nine times in the poem. The poet's reason for making so much of Agamemnon's story is twofold. First, during the course of the poem, he includes descriptions of the returns of all the major Trojan heroes, and this one is the most dramatic.

Second, the story is admirably suited for comparison with the story of Odysseus's return, as has been pointed out by D'Arms and Hulley, Post, and others.[19] The analogy is on more than one occasion made explicit: in Book i, 298–302, for example, Athene exhorts Telemachus to be as brave as Orestes; in iii the same com-

[19] Edward F. D'Arms and Karl K. Hulley, "The Oresteia-Story in the *Odyssey*," *Trans. Phil. As.* 77 (1946), *passim*; L. A. Post, "The Moral Pattern in Homer," *Trans. Phil. As.* 70 (1939), pp. 158–190.

parison is made by Nestor; in xi, Agamemnon contrasts Penelope and Clytaemnestra, and, even more interestingly, contrasts Odysseus's future reunion with his son to his own homecoming, in which he was deprived of the sight of *his* son. Why does Agamemnon make such a point of this, acting as if Clytaemnestra's greatest crime had been, not the double murder nor her adultery, but that she deprived him of a last sight of Orestes? Because the father–son relationship is the most important bond in the *Odyssey*; Odysseus's supreme success, to Homer, consists more in his possession of a good son, and secondarily of a good wife, than in his own heroism. The less attractive qualities of Agamemnon—seen so clearly in the *Iliad*—are entirely played down in the *Odyssey*, to make the comparison with Odysseus simple and clear.

The analogy is almost excessively straightforward: the evil Clytaemnestra is the opposite of the virtuous Penelope; Aegisthus is the same as the suitors (see i, 32–43)—although clearly warned, he brought about his own downfall through his own wickedness; Orestes is the same as Telemachus—he was a good son, who performed a courageous act of revenge; and finally, Agamemnon is the opposite of Odysseus—the latter lived most of his life with supreme success (xxiv, 24–5 "Son of Atreus, we used to say that you, of all our heroes, were the favorite for all time of Zeus the Thunderer") but fell in deepest tragedy, while the former, although he seemed ill-starred beyond all justice (e.g. xi, 216, "My child, unluckiest of mortals—"), was fated to end his sufferings in supreme success. And what does the Nekuia contribute to this pattern? Agamemnon's eulogy makes the comparison explicit and final; the story of Odysseus was not complete at the time of the other references to Agamemnon's tragedy; the question of Penelope's trustworthiness was not yet settled, Telemachus had not yet proved himself, and the suitors were still unpunished. But now, in the house of Hades, it is all over: justice has been done, the virtuous can be recognized, and the analogy—first brought up in Book i—is complete. It may perhaps be argued that this hammering-home of an already simple analogy is unnecessary and not very illuminating, but such a criticism would amount to a criticism of Homer himself, not of the Nekuia; the *Odyssey* is not a morally ambiguous tale like the *Iliad*; it is a melodrama in which heroes and villains are clearly defined, and to expect such a moralistic story not to drive its moral home is to ask for a different story altogether.

But what about Achilles? Unlike Agamemnon, his end was glorious. In the Nekuia, his splendid funeral is described at great length, and Agamemnon explicitly compares the hero's "blessedness" with his own misfortune. "Blessed son of Peleus, Achilles like to the gods—" says Agamemnon; a few speeches later he echoes those words with "Blessed son of Laertes, resourceful Odysseus." The comparison is clear; Achilles and Odysseus are alike in their happiness, in contrast to Agamemnon. Is one preferable to the other? Since Odysseus is listed second, there is perhaps an implication that his fortunes outshine those of the *Iliad*'s hero. There is no denying that, "like to the gods," Achilles is, in a sense, more divine, more brilliant than this "resourceful" human competitor, but so far as this poem is concerned, this contrast may also be in Odysseus's favor. In the rest of the poem, implied comparisons between Achilles and Odysseus can be detected in a number of instances, and (as opposed to the comparisons between Odysseus and Agamemnon, which are in terms of final success and domestic felicity) these comparisons are in terms of character, or rather, style of life.

For the famous Choice of Achilles was offered to Odysseus, too, as it is to every man. The decision which the hero of the *Iliad* made—for death and glory—is the simpler of the two ways. Telemachus (i, 237–40) mentions this possibility with envy: If Odysseus had died at Troy, he says, he would have had a splendid funeral and would have left me great glory to inherit. Odysseus himself echoes this sentiment in v (306, 311): "Thrice blessed, four times," he says, "were the Danaans who died on the broad fields of Troy. . . . would that I had died there. . . . I would have had my burial rites, and the Achaeans would have spread my fame. . . . " But as it is, Odysseus's lot—determined by his character—is not to die brilliantly in battle; his lot is to endure. He is not so glorious as Achilles, but he has patience, which Achilles did not have; he is flexible and resourceful, and he endures. He is not semidivine, like Achilles, but he is a man better equipped to deal with this world. Further, he *likes* this world; in the Calypso episode, he deliberately rejects divinity and embraces humanity with all its imperfections—Penelope is inferior to Calypso in beauty and stature, but the hero chooses her nonetheless; he is unashamed of his domesticity.

And is not this choice offered by Calypso practically identical with the more famous choice of Achilles? It is a question of divinity versus humanity, and Odysseus unhesitatingly makes a decision opposite to that of Achilles.

The two heroes had already been contrasted, and in the same way, in the *Iliad*. When Achilles wants to rush into battle at the climactic point of the epic (Book xix), the practical Odysseus restrains him. You are mightier than I, says Odysseus, but I am wiser than you; the army must eat first. This scene points up very nicely the difference between the two heroes—in it the whole character study of the *Odyssey* is already present in miniature. Achilles can do without food and drink, because he is scarcely human; Odysseus operates on a lower plane—he is the sort of man who can do servants' work and act the buffoon if it will serve his purpose—but, in the affairs of the world, he is right and Achilles is wrong; he speaks correctly when he says, "you are mightier but I am wiser."

In the poet's final evaluation, however, is Odysseus's kind of heroism actually seen as *better* than that of Achilles? Or are they (in the *Odyssey*) merely seen as two different ways of life, equally likely to produce final blessedness? Book xi seems to me to indicate Homer's bias. In his interview with the shade of Achilles, Odysseus says (483–6) "No man has ever been or will ever be more blessed than you. For while you were living the Argives honored you as a god, and now you are the mighty ruler of the dead down here." But Achilles impatiently denies this flattering tribute; I would rather be slave to a pauper on earth, he says, than king of all these corpses . . . but tell me about my son, and my father. . . . The order of these statements makes Homer's point clear. I think, Life itself is the most important thing; a glorious funeral is less to be desired than a fine son; Odysseus's human domesticity and self-preservation are better in the end than Achilles' divinity and glorious death. It is not, perhaps, a very noble point of view—but it is a lucid and sensible one, and just what we might expect from a bard who was able to find in the herding of pigs and the washing of dirty robes the stuff of poetry.

The second Nekuia is, of course, a doublet—we have already had one underworld scene—and this fact is the basis for some rather old-fashioned objections to the episode. But the *Odyssey* abounds in doublets: there are two cannibalism episodes; Calypso and Circe are somewhat similar; Leukothea and Eidothea are almost identical, and so on. The poet of the *Odyssey* apparently did not mind telling a good story twice, any more than he minded repeating a good turn of phrase. And in some of these doublets there is a significant difference, for example, in the two cannibalism episodes. In the Cyclops story, it is Odysseus's rashness (first in staying to explore the cave and meet its owner, next in boasting at the end of the scene) which brings trouble. In the Laestrygonian story, however, Odysseus shows that he has learned something about caution; he warily keeps his ship outside the cove while the others sail in; they are lost, and only his ship escapes. The two underworld scenes show a similar progress in knowledge; in the first, Agamemnon has learned the truth, and the hero of the *Odyssey* is found comparable to the hero of the *Iliad*.

The second Nekuia, then, serves at least five functions. It provides the third of three epitomes, which among them summarize the entire *Odyssey*. It provides an impressive panegyric for Penelope, who up till this point has not been properly rewarded. It provides the description of a funeral, which may have been a convention in *all* epics, or may simply be an echo of the *Iliad*. It provides a last bow for several major characters of the *Iliad* and the *Odyssey*: Hermes, the suitors, Achilles, Agamemnon, Menelaus, and Nestor. And it provides Homer's final evaluation of his hero, in comparison with Agamemnon and Achilles, the two chief characters of the *Iliad*. The scene may still be called poor, of course, but how can it be called irrelevant?

Bibliography

Austin, Norman. *Archery at the Dark of the Moon: Poetic Problems in Homer's Odyssey.* Berkeley and Los Angeles: University of California Press, 1975.

Clarke, Howard W. *The Art of the Odyssey.* Englewood Cliffs, N.J.: Prentice-Hall, 1967.

Fenik, Bernard. *Studies in the Odyssey.* Wiesbaden, West Germany: Steiner, 1973.

Finley, John. *Homer's Odyssey.* Cambridge: Harvard University Press, 1978.

Finley, M. I. *The World of Odysseus.* 2d rev. ed. London: Chatto and Windus, 1977.

Nelson, Conny, ed. *Homer's Odyssey: A Critical Handbook.* Belmont, Calif.: Wadsworth, 1969.

Page, Denys. *Folktales in Homer's Odyssey.* Cambridge: Harvard University Press, 1973.

_____ *The Homeric Odyssey.* Oxford: Clarendon Press, 1955.

Stanford, William Bedell, and Luce, John V. *The Quest for Ulysses.* New York: Praeger, 1974.

Stewart, Douglas J. *The Disguised Guest: Rank, Role, and Identity in the Odyssey.* Lewisburg, Pa.: Bucknell University Press, 1976.

Taylor, Charles H., Jr., ed. *Essays on the Odyssey: Selected Modern Criticism.* Bloomington: Indiana University Press, 1963.

Thornton, Agathe. *People and Themes in Homer's Odyssey.* London: Methuen, 1970.

Woodhouse, W. J. *The Composition of Homer's Odyssey.* 1930. Reprint. Oxford: Clarendon Press, 1969.

Notes on the Editor and Contributors

Howard W. Clarke, the editor, is Professor of Classics and Comparative Literature at the University of California, Santa Barbara, and the author of *Homer's Readers: A Historical Introduction to the Iliad and the Odyssey.*

Frederick M. Combellack, Professor Emeritus of Classics at the University of Oregon, has translated Quintus Smyrnaeus's *The War of Troy: What Homer Didn't Tell.*

Charles W. Eckert, Professor of English at Indiana University until his death in 1976, edited *Focus on Shakespearean Films.*

Jasper Griffin, Fellow of Balliol College, Oxford University, has written the Homer volume in Oxford University Press's "Past Masters" series.

Richmond Lattimore, Professor Emeritus of Greek at Bryn Mawr College, is the author of *Story Patterns in Greek Tragedy* and has published translations of Hesiod, Pindar, the Greek lyric poets and tragedians, the four Gospels, and Homer's *Iliad.*

William Bedell Stanford, formerly Regius Professor of Greek and now Pro-Chancellor of Trinity College of the University of Dublin, is the author of several books on classical and Irish subjects and has edited a number of Greek texts, including a two-volume *Odyssey.*

Dorothea Wender, head of the Classics Department at Wheaton College, has published an edition of *Roman Poetry, from the Republic to the Silver Age.*

Cedric H. Whitman, Eliot Professor of Greek at Harvard University until his death in 1978, published books on Sophocles, Aristophanes, and Euripides.